Who They Really Are:
A guide to being a spiritually aware parent from conception to the age of two.

Christina Fletcher

Copyright 2010

Second Edition- 2015 by Christina Fletcher

All rights reserved

Published and distributed by Castle Brae Publishing

Editorial supervision: Bryn Symonds

Front Cover photograph by Marc Millar photography
www.marcmillarphotography.com

With Special Thanks to Larah Bross and baby Millar.

All rights reserved. No part of this book may be reproduced by any mechanical, photographic, or electronic process, or in the form of phonographic recording; nor may it be stored in a retrieval system, transmitted, or otherwise be copied for public or private use- other than for "fair use" as brief quotations embodied in articles and reviews without prior written permission of the author.

The author of this book does not dispense medical advice or prescribe the use of a technique as a form of treatment for physical or medical problems without the advice of a physician either directly or indirectly. The intent of the author is only to offer information of a general nature to help you in your quest for emotional and spiritual well-being. In the event you use any of the information in this book for yourself, which is your right, the author and the publisher assume no responsibility for your actions.

Tradepaper ISBN 9780986874604

This book is dedicated to -

My Family

who provides me with the opportunity to Feel Good, to feel more relief than contrast and give me the platform to explore everything I really am.

You are wonderful spirits to play with.

Contents

Acknowledgements... 1

Introduction 3

Part One: Pregnancy

Chapter 1: The invitation and getting pregnant...... 15

    Exercises to release resistance................................. 18

    Affirmation.. 21

Chapter 2: First Trimester............................... 23

    Exercises to get to know yourself as the

    parent you will be... 27

    Affirmation 34

Chapter 3: Second Trimester........................... 35

    Baby as pure, positive Energy................................. 36

    Sounds and music, as your baby hears them........ 38

    Contact from your baby..39

    Exercises to get to know your baby................ 41

    Feeling good under the scrutinizing eyes of the

    Medical system....................................... 44

    Affirmation...47

Contents

Chapter 4: Third Trimester 49

    Labour and Delivery..50

    The Power of Energy 55

    Contemplating Breastfeeding 57

    Exercises to connect to your source and your baby...... 59

    Affirmation..61

Part Two: Infancy and Being the great provider

Special note for parents of special needs children 65

Special note for adoptive parents 67

Chapter 5: *First Month*

Pure Positive Being in Human Form

    Bask in your Now..69

    Becoming your baby's great provider 71

    Avoiding Hunger 73

    Colic, first pain, first contrasting experience 75

    Exercises... 78

    Affirmation 80

Contents

Special note on co-parenting 81

Chapter 6: *Second to sixth month*

Being the Great Provider

    What's happening in your baby's world 85

    Behavior 86

    Routine 88

    Health and Nutrition 91

    Meditation and back to Source 92

    Toys and Products 93

    You as parent, you as You 97

    Dealing with tiredness and living without sleep .. 99

    Affirmation 101

Chapter 7: *Sixth month to one year*

The Great Explorer

    What's happening in your baby's world 102

    Behaviour... 104

    Routine 108

    Health and Nutrition 111

    Sickness, colds and flus 114

    Meditation and back to Source 116

Contents

    Fun and Games 117

    Toys and Products.. 118

    Holidays and birthdays................................... 122

    You as parent, you as You 123

    Affirmation 127

Part Three: The Toddler Years

Chapter 8: *one to two years*

The Little Interpreter   131

    What's happening in your baby's world 132

    Behavior 135

    Routine 146

    Health and Nutrition 148

    Meditation and back to Source 150

    Fun and Games 152

    Toys and Products 156

    Holidays 158

    You as parent, you as You 160

    Affirmation... 165

Final Thoughts 167

Notes for Second Edition.......................................170

Acknowledgements

First, I would like to thank my husband, Jeff Fletcher, who is the king of my heart and the love of my life. You are my other half and it is because we are whole together that these words can flow. You've supported me, encouraged me, inspired me and taken silent, contemplative breaks with me when words weren't needed. I love you more than words could ever express.

Next, to my inspiration, our three darling children. Abigail, Giana and Frederick. You are the lights of my life and the joys of my heart. Each of you is so special to me, in your own, unique, wonderful, magical ways. Thank you for coming to us, for being the true spirits you are. I love everything You Really Are and it is because of you that this book has come into being.

To my Mom and Dad, the epitome of loving parents. What a great launching place you gave me. Thank you. I love you dearly.

Thanks to Bryn Symonds, who came out of nowhere and saved my neck. I am in awe of your generosity and courage in helping with this project, as well as the impeccable job you have done proofreading and editing. Thank you so much.

To Larah Bross, thank you for the wonderful photograph. You are beautiful. Welcome to the world, Billie Millar, it's a beautiful place to be.

Thanks also to Marc Millar (www.marcmillarphotography) for snapping the perfect moment of Larah and catching in the image of Who She Really Is, and then letting me use the result on the cover.

Who They Really Are

To my midwife nine years ago, who dared to call Abi "a little turnip" when I was pregnant with her. You spurred me to find a better way, straight from the beginning. Thank you so much.

To Esther and Jerry Hicks and Abraham, who gave me confirmations of what I was feeling and clarified it with words. Your inspiration did more than you could ever know. (Alright, Abraham, you probably know.)

To my Source, to God, and All I Really Am, I've been connected and disconnected over the years, thank you for the indicators to let me know the difference. Thanks for the contrast. Thanks for the heart-lifting rushes when connected. But most of all, thanks for making it so easy to get connected when I sit to write about spiritually aware parenting. Sometimes, the words would flow so easily, the next day I would be reading it for advice. So, thank you for using my fingers to flow through.

Introduction

To be a spiritually aware parent is one of the most rewarding experiences of life. It is to be present in your Now, and in your child's Now. It is to parent on a deeper level, and rather than just providing food and shelter, provide your child with everything You Really Are. It is to joyfully embrace the arrival of your baby and see him or her as Who They Are at their core and consciously bring them a joyful experience. It is a way for yourself to expand and grow as a person, and to share your day-to-day living with another being.

To be a spiritually aware parent is to create a home that is filled with joy, laughter and love. It is to avoid feeling like you are missing out on your own journey and then on the flip side, to feel that your child has slipped through your fingers when they are grown. Rather it is about being a co-creative, in-the-moment, conscious and understanding parent, who experiences joy and elation as your child experiences joy and vice versa. It is without sacrifice and without guilt.

It is a natural thing to be a parent. It is in our design. Our bodies are made to create and give birth, while our hearts yearn to love and nurture. Having children seems to fulfill us on both a logical and a magical level. Until you get pregnant, give birth and suddenly have to be responsible for a new human being. Suddenly images of colicky babies, bratty kids, minivans and stressed out parents rolling their eyes about their offspring seem to be the new reality that you find yourself hurtling towards. It seems that everyone enters parenthood with one idea, and more importantly their own idea, but by the time the child hits his first birthday it seems easiest to just slip into what everyone else does to get the results you need to keep going.

But this goes against the spiritual resurgence that has been occurring in our world. Now, more than ever before, people are aware. Aware of spirit, aware of Bliss, aware of magic, and aware of creating a life that you dream of everyday rather than reacting to everything that fills your experience. As an individual you are steering your ship, but now that you have a child coming into your life, how do you become spiritually aware for two? How do you remain You, who *you* really are, while trying to raise them? How do you let them be Who They Really Are while trying to be in control?

This book is about being the parent you want to be. It's about seeing your child, and all children, as the pure, positive spiritual beings They Really Are. It is about remaining true to the

Introduction

Spiritual Being you are, and as that, expanding and enjoying the magical experiences of parenthood.

We are pure, positive energy beings. That is to say that there is another part of us larger than this physical human form. Call it a soul, a spirit, a higher self, The Real Me. It is the part of us that is connected to Source or God. In fact it is God. When we act from the perspective of the spirit, we feel good and things go well. It often feels when we act from spirit that we are children on a playground; we might have a few falls but they don't stop us from jumping to the next swing or slide for another exhilarating time. Our emotions and how we feel at every moment are indicators of how close to our spirit self we are. As the spirit is only positive energy (there is no dark side, no evil, no force of bad, just lack of light) then when we feel positive emotion, we are close to Home. Joy, happiness, excitement, anticipation, fulfillment, appreciation, ease and contentment even hope are the levels of being spirit based, whereas frustration, anger, bitterness, boredom, fed-upness, hatred are far from Who We Really Are.

However, we do experience Contrast, meaning bad days, awkward situations or irritating people. The Contrast lets us know what we don't want so we know what we do want. Even when we experience a negative emotion, it lets us know that we aren't being Ourselves so it gives us a reason to find a thought that feels better and get back Home. Contrast also, by making us know what we do want, makes us set forth a desire for something different. Our spirit receives this message loud and clear and literally becomes it, then waits for us to get over our frustration, anger or OFF feeling and readjust to the perspective of Spirit. When we then act from that perspective, we feel good again, and the Law of Attraction is ready to kick in with something to resolve what we were so frustrated with. After all, when we and our Spirits act as one, there is no stopping what is possible.

The Law of Attraction has been a huge topic lately, especially for people who know they don't have what they want and find out they can attract it into their lives. But often this comes from an "I want" state, which can be based in frustration. If you aren't acting from Source, the law of attraction will only give more frustration, not what you are trying to set forth. As I have explained it to our children, we are like giant magnets, and our emotions are what those magnets attract. If we are angry, we are saying to God, "I'm feeling angry. I'm not stopping this feeling." And God says, "Oh, ok. They want to experience anger. That's the message we're getting by what they are radiating. So let's give them more of what they are asking for." This can be every time you walk around feeling bitter, frustrated, full of self-pity, unloved, or even broke. It is the message being sent out. However, when you bound down the street in joy, when you laugh, sing and love or when you are focused on appreciating what you have, when you love everything and everyone around you, (or at least find positive aspects of them to focus on) then you feel good. God or Source energy recognizes itself and gives you more things to feel that same joy about.

Feel Good = more to feel good about. Feel Bad = more to feel bad about.

Introduction

These are powerful basements to approach Spiritual Parenting. Children are born knowing only they are pure, positive beings. Contrast starts right away with every hunger pain, every tooth coming in, every tummy ache, even every time Mom and Dad aren't in the room. We as parents introduce the gap of being Spirit and being human, and how we react to those moments, and how far we let that gap widen, can set them on their feet running as they grow up, determined to stay true to their own Spirits.

As a parent, it is an empowering thing to parent from your Spirit perspective. To make sure that you grab those brief moments to make yourself feel better makes you see things more clearly, makes you respond naturally, rather than react to what your children are bringing to the day. It also slows things down, allowing you to enjoy your parenting experience, not see it as a burden, or as a step away from your own life.

Throughout this book I will talk about feeling good or finding a feeling good place. It is important that when I say feeling, that that is what you read. Your thoughts are the keys to your emotional state, and in return your emotions reflect what you've been thinking all day long. We as a society have gotten into the habit of losing control of our own thoughts. We react to what happens around us, we watch horrible things on TV, read about tragedies in the newspaper, and then we re-live it over and over again through our thoughts. Thoughts are like sound waves and their vibration is what the Law of Attraction responds to. It is also what your emotions are reflecting.

So consider finding a feeling good place as a good short cut. Start to see what thoughts occupy your time. Are you feeling content, happy and joyful? What thoughts make you feel that way? How often do you counteract the effect of those thoughts by adding a subtext, such as "I love it when the sun is shining. Too bad it rains so often where we live." Do you resist feeling good? When you read the words *Feel Good*, do thoughts like "well if everyone just did what feels good the world would go into chaos" pop into your head?

Don't read *Feel Good* as "do whatever you feel like." That is not the point. The idea here is to focus on what you are feeling first, before doing anything. It is only when you are jiving, when you are exhilarated, content, connected, yourself that inspired action comes. When you act out of resentment, frustration, boredom or anger, the result of your action will never make you feel any different and that is the action that leads to a chaotic world.

You cannot have a happy end to an unhappy journey.

Therefore, stop trying.

When I say Feel Good, which trust me I'll be saying a lot, then it's inviting you to stop in your tracks and *Feel* Good. Feel good to your core. Focus on it until you get that lilt in your heart, that lovely rush down your spine, that natural feeling of wellbeing pouring over you.

How do you get that on command? You find a thought that feels fantastic. Actually create a mental bagful of thoughts that feel fantastic. Remind yourself of them in whatever way feels comfortable to you: images, journaling, lists, inspiration boards, boxes of photos, even writing them up and down your arm. Focus on what you have, feel the satisfaction of appreciating where your life is right now, imagine what you want to experience in the future. Resist the idea of naming the

Introduction

thing in your head, checking it off as "Feel Good thought done" and then picking up in the same feeling place where you left off. Practice your feeling good thoughts. Use the power of your imagination and feel your thoughts with every one of your senses. Be *In* your thoughts and feel the joy rush over you.

Feel the wellbeing.

Yes, this takes listening to how you feel and re-lighting the fire of your imagination. Both, unfortunately, are things that are often suppressed by parents. Both, we are often taught to "grow out of." Both, as a spiritually aware parent, you will want to encourage and support within your own children. For out of the imagination can come joyful thoughts, and out of joyful thoughts come joyful experiences, and out of joyful experiences, a joyful life. And that is what every parent wants for their child.

Now, the great thing about using your thoughts to inspire a feeling of joy is that you don't need to have anyone or anything change for you to feel better. So often we blame outside influences for how we feel. Now you can switch it on its head and feel better and things will change. This is good news as a parent, or even as a soon to be parent. Switching focus from morning sickness, labor, colic or a tantrum, and grounding yourself first with a few moments of feeling good will change the way you see things. When you put your focus back on the problem, you might find it looks different now that you feel different.

Another thing I will be mentioning a lot is breathing and taking the time to breathe properly.

Who They Really Are

We are born knowing how to breathe properly. Your baby will be born breathing properly. His tummy will rise and fall with every breath he takes as his diaphragm expands like a balloon to fill his lungs with air. However, by the time he is two months old, you will notice he breathes faster, his chest filling up rather than it dropping to his navel. This is true for most of us. However, learning how to breathe naturally will ground you, refocus you and bring you back to Who You Really Are. Anyone who has done yoga or taken singing lessons will know this. I encourage you to practice it frequently. If you are pregnant, there is no greater tool for labour or for a feeling of wellbeing than breathing, and in using it after your baby is born, you will feel more in the moment, and more Yourself. You will act rather than re-act.

To breathe naturally, focus first on your breathing and consciously send it down towards your belly button, let the air fill you up and your middle section fill like a balloon. Then exhale slowly, letting the balloon collapse naturally. Never force your tummy to rise, and take your time on both the in and the out breathes. Even doing this three or four times in a row will make you feel better.

In each section of this book you will notice some time dedicated to practicalities of raising children. Nutrition to discipline, medical attention to baby supplies will be looked at as well as the more obvious "spiritual" topics like meditation and behavior. The reason for this is simple: we are still physical beings and no matter what, our experiences in this physical body affect our spirit and how we feel. For instance, I know it is likely for me to get cranky when I'm thirsty; therefore, even

Introduction

water can move me closer to Who I Really Am. Hunger, unbalanced diets, or food colorings can artificially disconnect your children, and without awareness to that possibility, it is easy to run around in circles trying to be a spiritually aware parent. Also, it's been my experience that through what the world offers in toys and baby equipment, we often run the risk of falling into trends rather than listening to our inner instincts. When you are choosing to be Aware and answerable to no one but your Source as a parent, it is vital to be aware of all aspects of your child's world.

Now, a bit of a background check. I was raised as a Christian, but with a mystical approach. I had conflicting feelings as a child as I could experience a personal God, but Christian dogma confused me with how it all fits in. I was a seeker and wanted it to all make sense. I loved feeling God, sitting on a swing, staring at the stars, singing with the birds. I invented prayers and meditations at about 11 and would lock myself in the bathroom with the lights off to try them out, much to my family's annoyance and discomfort. However, then I would try to fit in the stuff other people were telling me about God, and felt at odds with it all. Was I doing it wrong? I continued this approach up to my early 20s when after even religious studies in university couldn't provide the answers I needed, I threw caution to the wind and committed myself to listening to my inner voice, my God, my spirit, my instincts. Suddenly magic started to happen. I met my husband, my soulmate, on an inspired trip to England and a few months later I was pregnant with our first daughter.

Since then, my husband and I have been inspired by the works of Abraham Hicks, Deepak Chopra, Neale Donald Walsch as well as many others.

I had always been eager to pass on an understanding of spirituality to children, but without the framework of a religion to call on, I found myself unsupported. No picture books, no movies, no structured beliefs. Suddenly, I had to trust only on when things felt right to talk about it, or not to talk when it felt really *off*. I had to trust that it would be inspired, and I would be shown how. After many trials and errors of not listening, I finally let it become the most inspiring journey of my life. Now, every time I hear our children laugh and sing, I know that we are doing exceptionally well together on this journey of life.

We might as well enjoy the ride, and that's what this book is about: Feeling Good and helping your children feel the same. In doing so, you will attract only the best feeling things into your life and you will experience joy every day. What could be better than that?

Part One:
Pregnancy

Who They Really Are

A guide to being a spiritually aware parent

Chapter One:

Invitation and Difficulties getting Pregnant

I'm not going to make concrete comments on why someone can't get pregnant or stay pregnant. This is only what I've observed and what, on a spiritual ground, might help. There are many reasons why someone might not be able to get pregnant. However, as this is a book that sees the mind as the builder, I believe that these problems are more symptoms of something that goes deeper. Each individual's life is different, but something like the following thought process could have a blocking effect.

Who They Really Are

"I think a baby would really set my life on course. I'm getting older and I'm running out of time. I don't mind waking up in the middle of the night or changing diapers. I really want a baby. Why can't I have a baby? There are so many unwanted pregnancies, and here I want one so badly. Something must be wrong with me. There is something wrong with me. I'll never have a baby. I'll never have that bond. I want that bond, but I'll never have that. I want someone to come running into my arms, to come to me for help. Why does no one want me?"

There is nothing wrong with you and everything is perfect. The question naturally arises as to do you really want a baby? And your answer will of course be YES! said angrily and slamming the book in my face. But your life might not be a mirror of that. Is this the magnet you are holding up? Remember, it's the feeling of our thoughts that set out what we are going to attract. You can repeat, "I want a baby, I want a baby, I want a baby," as often as you want, but if the focus is on the lack of baby in your life, you better get use to it.

What are your reasons for wanting to be pregnant? It's easy to spew off the common phrases like wanting to be needed or wanting to experience the bond, but are you actually in a state of inviting someone else into your life? Also, adding the stress of limited time puts pressure on you and focus on the lack of a child. Comparing yourself to others' experiences lowers your feeling place to one of despair and frustration, as does noticing the lack of being depended upon and having a close bond. If the image of someone running to you stirs up sadness within you, due to the lack of it in your life, then you will attract sadness around that situation into your experience.

Do you see children as just that, *children*? What I mean is: do you see them as all the same, with the same milestones in learning and in behavior? How would you react if your child past these milestones at different times than everyone else? Do you see kids as kids or as individuals, who, as spiritual beings, decide to take on a human form, growing and exploring for reasons of expansion and learning. We say they grow up, but they don't. None of us do, not on a soul level. Life is a progression of learning and expanding; it's just that as children we start from a different vantage point. There is so much to learn from a child exploring the little wonders in life that we take for granted. Each child is an individual consciousness, and within that first year they are forming their own thoughts and opinions of the world around them. Even as an infant they are their own personality, their own spirit of pure positive energy. They are just as prominent in personality and spirit before they are born as we are here and now in this adult state. The growing years are simply about forming opinions and interpreting the world around them in order to start having the contrast and desire to want more, experience more and expand more.

So, rather than being ready to change diapers and dedicate years to taking care of a child, are you ready to aid and assist the expansion of someone who comes forth and wants to try things? Even if it's not in the way you want or expect? Are you ready to expand yourself within the relationship of another being? Are you ready to have another person in your life, for all your life, to love and be loved? YES! you shout.

Therefore, I suggest these exercises to anyone who tells me they want to get pregnant.

Exercise One

Write a letter to your unborn child inviting it into your life. Build that bond now. Imagine what they would be like, what it would be like to have them around. Write that you love them already and that whenever they want, you are ready to be their mother. Write it semi-unconsciously. Don't re-read and make corrections, just let it flow through you. Let it be from your heart and a true expression of who you are as You and as a Parent. Don't judge yourself. Offer yourself up as a parent just as you are. This can even be a journal, so write something everyday, even good-nights and good-mornings. Not only will you feel that bond already, you will have a great guide to look back on when that baby is in your arms.

Exercise Two

Pick up a doll for a week, and keep it as an infant. I know, you might have to go to work, or a shop, but chances are if you say to co-workers, *"I think I would like to have a baby and I'm testing it out to see if it feels good to me,"* or *"I want a baby and I'm changing my experience of this so that I know what its like and the Law of Attraction will recognize it,"* they will respect you for it. Maybe you'll start a trend.

Or leave it with someone else while you go out. Although, ask yourself what you would do if it was a living baby, because if you would leave it in care already, then maybe there isn't room yet.

Exercise Three

Talk to your partner about parenting and how they feel about it. What are their experiences with children, were they positive or negative, how would they do things differently? Go through major life discussions like education, sex, death, God, and how you would approach them together as parents. It might release some resistance.

Exercise Four

Write a list of the things you love about your life now. Your creative power is in the Now. Write down every little thing that you appreciate in your life, even your special brand of toothpaste or having a good hair day. By focusing on your feeling good now, you will attract more things to make you feel good. That is the Law. Therefore, even if your attention wanders from "Baby" or "No Baby," the Powers that Be will recognize what else will make you feel good and bring it on. Therefore, Feel Good in the Now!

Exercise Five

Talk to your partner about having children. Is this is a joint passion? My husband has always known when we got pregnant. He has always "sent up with intention" even if it was just a subconscious thing. It was as if he and the baby connected first before getting me involved. He gathered the energy and then released it to me. Just because the woman carries the baby for nine months in no way diminishes the connection between the father and the baby. After all, in gardening we say the plants come from the seed, not from the soil it grew in. So talk to your partner about his role to Invite and then Release.

If you have just experienced a miscarriage or if you have a history of miscarriage(s), it is important to come to terms with them and not have them continually thrust you out of a feeling good space when you think of pregnancy and when you want to try again. Of course, any loss in pregnancy is gut-wrenching; I'm not saying it's not. I'm just saying that as it reminds you of sadness, you will be holding up the sadness magnet and attracting more. You have to alter your perspective in order to attract a different result. Therefore, although it is so easy to go through a mirage of ideas of what went wrong and often look to yourself as the one at fault, trust me when I say, nothing went wrong. The outcome was not what you wanted, or even expected, but there were two involved here, and no, I don't mean your partner. You have been part of a soul journey. Someone wanted to experience just the first few weeks of human life. You were the ground to do that in and it thanks you sincerely. This loss doesn't create any absolute about any future pregnancy. It was an individual's experience and you have been woven into it. It is okay to feel a little bit better at anytime you feel ready. Take your experience as it is, and was. Even write a letter to the child who will not be born to you in a few months, and invite it to come back at anytime. Tell it there will always be great love here for it, in its physical form or any other form it would wish to visit in.

Then I suggest doing loads of things unfitting for a pregnant woman, from fast-food to skydiving, whatever makes you totally exhilarated, and savour every minute of it.

Affirmation

I stand here waiting for you, dear one. My arms are open and my heart is full of love for Who You Really Are. You do not have to be in my arms to exist. I know you are out there. I know we are intertwined. If I close my eyes, I can feel your essence. I will spend more time with that essence of All you are, just because it feels so lovely having you in my life on some level. I trust your timing, for you have no impatience. Your timing is perfect. Know that I love you, know I am here for you, and know that I am ready and willing to be a portal for you. Until you are ready I will take part in the blissful expectation. Like the trees in the winter waiting for their first leaves to bud, I will slumber in the sweet knowledge that you are there. We are, and always will be connected.

A guide to being a spiritually aware parent

A guide to being a spiritually aware parent

Chapter Two:

First Trimester

Well, so it begins. Planned or a surprise, you are pregnant. A soul has chosen you as their portal into human form. You are their bouncing off place to experience this wonderful life. For the next nine months your body will be co-occupied. Parenting starts now and approached well, you can start a bond that will last a lifetime.

Without much confidence at the time, but a satisfying confirmation after birth, I have always gotten to know our children well before they were born. I've known before tests that I was "occupied" and more than myself. I've started talking to and welcoming the baby. What's even more exciting, I've closed my eyes and been filled with the wonderful feeling of who they are, their essence, and then recognized it when I've laid eyes on them for the first time.

So much happens at this time. Every cell in your body jumps to attention and starts fulfilling its mission, what it was made to do. *The best thing any expectant mother can do is not worry.* Cells are affected by you, how you feel, your stress, your beliefs. So sit back, eat what you think is right and healthy, so you feel like you are helping, trust that your body finds this as natural as breathing. Also, trust that your baby has chosen its experience. This is not only about you anymore. Although we are accustomed to thinking of babies as helpless, they are deliberately experiencing life even through pregnancy. Even with miscarriages, it is safe to say that the soul has decided that this was all they needed to experience to move on to something different.

So make this pregnancy a happy time in your heart and mind. Tell yourself how it's only for nine months, and your body will naturally return to its previous form later on. If people tell you about their pregnancy experiences, remind yourself that that is exactly what it was, *their* experience. Yours can and will be totally different. But more about that in a minute. Delivery is after the pregnancy and that is where your basement of your experience is laid.

If only there were more situations in life that gave you a nine-month prep time. These nine months can be so delicious if you choose your focus carefully and make it magical. I'm not one to get into flowery dialogue. I'm not going to talk about the beauty of a pregnant woman, or the romanticism of sharing your body with another being, all of which may or may not ring true to you. Rather, I walk a tightrope between the magic of the time and the practicalities that will pave your road for a spiritual parenthood. This is the time when you know you are going to experience parenthood, you know another person is coming into your life, you know that certain responsibilities are coming your way. That might fill you with nervousness, it might freak you out, it might fill you with joy, but this is the time when you can come to terms with that.

I always feel that the first trimester is about adjustment, getting to know yourself as a mother. The second is about getting to know your unborn baby, and the third is about both of you bonding and preparing to create a good birth. These time frames of course overlap, but for this purpose let's look at each trimester. If you've read any pregnancy book (and God knows I read a lot of them) this is the usual form.

"Oh my GOD!" is the first response. Joy, elation, excitement, or often panic, tears and running to the bathroom, the second. I was lucky enough to always be excited and so was my husband. We never gave a care to if there was enough money or whether it was convenient. Rather, we knew we were the lucky ones because we'd been chosen. Someone saw the love we had, and decided they wanted to be part of it. This is the view that rang true with me. I invite you to try it on for size, but if it doesn't fit, then hunt around for a good feeling thought about it. Don't stick a happy face on the situation and pretend everything is fine when you don't feel it is. Rather, spin your perspective around a few times to get a better feeling one.

Why? This is a time to make yourself feel as good as you can as often as you can. This is a time to look at your thoughts and make them matter. This is a time to feel good, and if not good, then better than bad. When you feel fear, focus on the love, when you feel sick, focus on the well, when you feel sad or hormonal, grab a funny movie, or focus on a sunset. Feel less stressed if not relaxed! The reason is simple. You want a good pregnancy and a good delivery and your thoughts can help with that. As I said at the beginning of the chapter, your thoughts affect every cell in your body. Your cells in your body know precisely what they need to do, and it is your thoughts that can prevent them from doing their job. Even in labor, stress and resisting the flow of nature is a huge cause of things going wrong. Clinically it has been proven that not letting a woman find her own comfortable position and follow her inner instincts leads to complications. So, let your instincts and inner knowledge be heard right from the get-go and by the time you get to delivery you will know what to listen to. This is the perfect time to get to know yourself and to get to know how to listen to the deep inner voice which comes from Source.

So, get on this ride. You're on it anyway, but you can really be on it, or let it take you kicking and screaming. Personally, I've always liked being on the nine-month rollercoaster.

It is a myth that your life will no longer be your own. You are still You and having a baby doesn't alter this; if anything it amplifies it. Didn't you hate it when your mother refused to let you grow up? Didn't it frustrate you when you felt you were her only life and your leaving the nest was cutting her lifeline? So right now refuse to give that feeling to your child. I hate to break it to you, but technically you are merely a portal for this child to come into this world. Your life, your world are still as much yours as ever. And that is just what you and your child want. The best thing you can teach your child is through the example of yourself. Show them your inspirations, your dreams, your struggles, or lessons, your experiences for that is why your baby chose you. To be able to look at your child and for them to know you are doing your best at being You is a powerful and inspiring thing. So start now. That's why the first trimester is so important. It's quiet enough for you to hear yourself, and not too busy in your abdomen for you to get distracted. It's a great way to feel you're doing something healthy while your body is doing so much work without your input.

But what does it mean to get to know yourself?

Well, up to this point you've formed thoughts and ideas about things. You've got opinions and beliefs, but chances are, except in discussions with others, they didn't come to the forefront of your day-to-day life. Good mood, bad mood, sure your partner could read them and help with them, but it didn't really matter. You didn't have to really decide how you wanted to live, because you only had yourself to please. What an exciting time for self-defining and fine-tuning! Also, it's a great time to look at your life as a child. Remembering how you felt as a child is a parenting tool that is invaluable. It is the difference between being a by-the-book parent and being an emotionally involved one.

A few exercises to get this ball rolling. I suggest getting a good notebook for this. It will provide you with a great handbook to look back on.

Exercise One

Write a timeline of your own life. How did you get from there to here? Go back to when you were born. What's your earliest memory? Don't write a lot, just bullet points outlining important dates or years starting from when you were born. Sketch out each period as they get clearer in your mind. This merely acts as a guide, but a guide to many things. First, it will show that your life has been a journey up to this point, but definitely not ending at this point. This will just be another experience to add to the collection you have already started. Second, it will show you your opinion of important details of your childhood. And third, it will show how your childhood affected your life after it.

Exercise Two

When you have your timeline, go to the start and look at your childhood. What is the first feeling that comes to mind? It could be "That was a great childhood," or "I hated my childhood," or somewhere in between. Then to put yourself in a better feeling place, ask yourself to recall some of your favourite memories. Focus on the good stuff. Mother memories are interesting because they give you an idea whether you thought your mother did the kind of job you would like to give your child. Write these down in freeform just to go as deep as you can. This is a private journal so say whatever comes to the top of your head. If it helps, do a page with the heading "Things I want my child to experience," and then another "Things I don't want my child to experience."

Exercise Three

Sticking in your childhood for one last exercise, close your eyes and imagine yourself as that child again. Not in any specific situation, but imagine how you felt. Imagine how you saw the world, what you loved, what excited you, what terrified you. As an example, remember being excited about getting a soda out of a vending machine? Well as a small child this was probably magic to you. Remember a $5 bill feeling like you were rich or a hill being exciting because it was so good to roll down. Children have the amazing capability to find the magic in everything and by remembering how this feels you turn yourself into the parent that says, "Wow, that's amazing honey!" and re-live the wonder of it all over again, rather than just being the parent in a department store yelling, "Stop dawdling and don't be stupid." The world is a true magical wonder and we are so lucky to have children there to remind us of it.

However, sometimes simple things terrify them and it is important to remember what that was for you as well. This will make you sensitive to those fears and not a parent who makes scary demands on your child without knowing it. So what were you afraid of, how was it dealt with and how did you get over it? Create a storage room in your memory of things that made you unmoveable with fear. As a child, that feeling is overwhelming. Soon, you will see your baby get his first fears, around 5-6 months, and you will have more compassion, more in-the-moment sensitivity, if you remember that fear is real to your child, not an inconvenience to you.

My husband and I always laugh about it, but he watched monster movies too young and was scared and I watched murder mysteries too young and was terrified. Therefore, we both were so aware of what our children watched, they were lucky to watch anything! But still, our children have very few bad dreams or scary thoughts and it is reassuring to know that if they do, we can draw on our mental storage to help shift focus, find the root cause or at least sympathize.

So, what rocked you as a child? What made you scared? What filled you with wonder? What did you like to do? What shows did you watch? What toys did you play with? Did you like to be hugged or kissed best? Did you want to be hugged or kissed? What were you jealous of? What did you love, love, love? What did you feel good about? What did you give up on? How did you feel around family? What filled you with a sense of awe, of something bigger than you? The list goes on and on. Play with this, it can be an eye opener and an endless supplier of information you will draw on for years to come. Some of the most successful times with our children come from when we have gone to this inner storeroom of knowledge and understood our children better. From crafts and movies we loved and have passed down, to remembering how it feels to feel insecure around family, or shy in a crowd, talking to your child from a place of "I remember that feeling" is a great basement for any parent.

Exercise Four

Look at a few major topics of life, such as your beliefs about God, life, death, sex, and love. Do you like where you are in those beliefs? Are you in a religion, and are you defined by it? Do you want to pass it on to your child, or is there a natural pull in you to chart out a different course? You don't need to have all the answers now, so this isn't to cause stress, rather it's interesting to watch yourself on the topics. Don't worry. The right words will come when your child is ready to hear them. However, this is a good door opener to getting to know who you are.

Exercise Five

Take a moment outside, and breathe in deep. Start practicing breathing properly so that your tummy rises with your diaphragm expanding to fill your lungs with air. Breathe in and out naturally. Anyone who has any vocal training knows this technique, but it is also common in yoga. Breathe in through your nose and let the air travel to your navel. Don't stretch it to discomfort, rather just let the balloon fill and drop slowly, releasing the air through your mouth. Concentrate on this breathing technique by just focusing on your breath as it flows through you. Get the hang of it now as in a few months you won't see your tummy rise, but your baby will get the benefit of it. It is also the famous breathing technique from Lamazze classes and will definitely help you in labour. However, now it is wonderful to ground you in Who You Really Are as well as calm you, and focus you. Continue this technique throughout pregnancy and after your child is born as a quick and easy re-focusing practice. You will notice your baby naturally breathes like this when he is first born and continues to do so for the first month. It is only after getting use to a different pace of life that this natural instinct leaves. Get back to your natural state by practicing this deep breathing. It truly connects you to All That You Really Are.

Who They Really Are

Whenever you do one of these exercises, be aware of how you feel. If you visit a negative childhood memory during one of the recollection exercises, come out of the remembrance with thoughts that feel good. Don't hang around in the feeling of your past all day. Simply revisit it and then do a rampage of appreciation on your Now. This can be on anything you love or that makes you feel better. Do it with a steady flow. Even if it starts off with "I'm so glad that's over with." For instance here's one of mine.

"I love where I am now. I love my husband. I love our home. I love the way we make our house ring with laughter. I love writing, and reading what's been written. I love children. I love building up a child. I love building up anyone. It's a great feeling to make someone feel good, to see them feel better than they did. I love to sing. Look at that sunset. I love the sun. I love it in summer when it feeds every cell in my body. I love my body. I love the way my lungs take care of my breathing without my thinking about it, and the way my heart pumps blood through all my veins even though I didn't tell them to. I love the way my body can make a baby in the same way. I love this time in my life and I can't wait to see what miracles unfold themselves in my path."

These exercises can be done as often as you want or just once if you don't like the experience. I believe it is important to do them with your partner as well. This sort of appreciation spiel can truly set your day and henceforth your pregnancy truly on course. To bounce them off another person and vice versa is a true combustion of positive energy, which leaves both of you feeling refreshed. If there's anything I suggest that I hope will catch on, it's that this kind of appreciation thought process will start to be done by everyone. There is no better way to get out of bed and no better way to go to sleep.

One last note on the first trimester. Get into the habit of listening to your instincts. I can think of no time in your life when you will hear more of other people's opinions, from family, doctors or total strangers. Everyone wants to give you their take. But you know how you are doing. You know that relaxing in the wellbeing of everything you are will make this a great experience. You know your baby will experience whatever it set out to do. Don't fall into the first trimester trap of wondering if you should tell anyone until you reach week 13 because that's what people say as a "just in case." Embrace it fully, and trust Source, yourself, your body, your baby's freewill, and nature.

Who They Really Are

Affirmation

Breathe and allow. Breathe and allow. Every cell in my body knows its job right now. In fact each one was made to do this. To me, making a baby's body seems like a mammoth task, but to my body it is as simple as making my lungs breathe and my heart beat. It takes no effort from me. Knowing this, I trust in my body and all the unseen forces that make things happen. My only role in this is to Love. I love my coming adventures. I love the spirit that will occupy this growing body within me. I am growing too. I am growing into a mother. I will not be defined as a mother, but I will fill out to being a mother. Love is the power force behind my growth. As I breathe deeply, I will allow my new motherhood to flow over me. I feel no limitation, no restriction. Rather, it is a new vantage point, a new perspective that will only bring good into my life.

Chapter Three

Second Trimester

This is my favourite time of a pregnancy. For one thing you know by now, I mean deeply know, that you are pregnant, and you've come to terms with it. Also, you will start to show, or you will have by the end of this trimester, and with that comes all sorts of amazing moments for you to thrill at.

One of the most miraculous things happens around 13 weeks. Your placenta is fully functioning and the baby is being taken care of by a new part of you. Isn't it amazing that you have grown a new organ? Not only that, but it will feed and nurture your baby for the rest of your pregnancy as well as provide immunity protection from things you are exposed to. This is the ultimate "universal manager" made physical in your body to take care of everything. Anyone who is studying spirituality in any manner knows that trust or faith in something greater than yourself is ultimate. God, Source, Higher Being, well here it is folks. This is your baby's lifeline and it has been grown inside of you as a provider, nurturer and Great Protector. That is something to bask in.

For my first two pregnancies, I didn't fully appreciate the placenta, but by my third I understood its power and sometimes was overwhelmed by it, yet so thankful. I would take a moment here or there to just pass the wellbeing of our child to this great source. Any body that can make this great organ will find it no problem to create a magnificent child. You can have faith in that.

Baby as Pure, Positive Energy

I want to introduce to you the idea of your child as a Spiritual Being, as it hovers in and out of your body, experiencing what you experience, hearing what you hear and say. Let's look at the perspective of this being. The idea of it will not only help now, but after your baby is born and into their childhood.

Imagine for a moment Pure positive energy, without any negative thought or emotion. It observes life on Earth, experiences its joy and probably marvels at its discord. Then in that joy it witnesses two people making love, and part of that whole decides it would like to experience life from that starting point, through the vantage point of those people. I'm not going to go into the discussion of when or how it enters human form, but it has chosen you to do it through. I'm sure it knows the experiences you are ready to offer. Now here in its second trimester, this spirit can really start to experience its physical form. In you there is a baby's body and with each arm and leg movement someone else is experiencing that. It can hear your voice and the tone in which you speak. It is beginning to feel the contrast of life, knowing pain, even just emotional pain, when you get upset or stressed. It can feel the connection back to where it came from when you feel joy, excitement, passion or love. Imagine its thrill when it receives words from you directly to it? If it has come from a Pure Positive Source, then your Pure Positive Attention would feel like being Home. There would be no gap from there to here, which is literally what we are all striving for all our lives on this planet. We fill our lives with so much contrast to this sometimes, yet when we experience Joy and Love we feel connected again to that great Source.

In the world of a baby, simplicity is key. I'll be saying that a lot over the next few chapters. It's really a matter of Connected and not connected. As it grows up over its first year, it will try to broaden and experience more of the not connected to feel greater satisfaction with Connected. But right now, this is as unconnected as it wants to be.

With this picture in your mind, doesn't it suddenly take on great importance to feel good? Isn't it vital to strive to find that joy over little things, and limit frustrations and friction to a minimum? Therefore, if you don't want to do the dishes, don't right now. Take time to bathe in a good feeling thought. If someone is nagging at you, tell them you don't wish for your baby's ears to hear it and seeing as it can't leave the room, you will have to. Take care of yourself.

Enjoy this time. It is one of exploration. Through the first trimester you accustomed yourself to the idea of parenthood, now try it on, have fun with it. Talk to your baby all the time. When you eat something delicious, comment out loud with, "Oh, I can't wait for you to try this." When you see something beautiful, say or think, "I wish you could see this. I'll try to show it to you one day." Take each of the experiences of your day from the new perspective of your baby, who is eager to see everything from its new point of view and share in its excitement. Can you imagine having a bag over your head and being sent to a different country only to be told you had to wait nine months to see anything? You would be so eager. That excitement is a wonderful feeling, so grab hold of it and feel great.

Sounds and music as your baby hears them

After my 16-week ultrasound with our first daughter, I received a CD where I heard what sound was like inside the womb. It showed various examples, such as music and conversation. Conversation is interesting because it is important to watch tones. But this is also very true for music. Start to listen to music and conversational tones from your baby's perspective. Once you feel the baby's movement, you'll have a good idea how it affects them, but even before that, imagine and watch how it affects you.

This is the basis of the Mozart Effect. I'm not the strongest advocate of this process, which is the theory that Mozart's music stimulates brain cells and can make your unborn baby smarter. However, music is a powerful medium and as somebody who is watching how you feel and how to keep in a feeling good place, it is an important thing to be attentive to what you listen to. As an ex-musical therapist, I've experienced the affect of music on a person first hand.

So, really ask yourself what music makes you feel good? What makes you want to dance, to sing, to laugh? Classical music might not be your thing, so don't feel it's a have to. Your baby will sense your aggravation if that's what it stirs in you. But its quality is its soothing capabilities and its pace. For my last pregnancy, our girls had just fallen in love with Abba and it was ringing through the house all the time. We wondered what effect this would have on our poor son, but he's the happiest baby I know. Also, I would use the softer songs as lullabies after he was born and it made continuity. Listen to the lyrics in songs. For instance a Hard Rock or Rap song filled with words of anger, could not make you really feel good, no matter how it makes you dance. How would your baby react to Eminem? Love songs, silly songs, light songs? Keep a sense of love and laughter about it. Remember that your baby is hearing it all the time. Start looking through your favourite music and pick out favourites for lullabies. Babies love to be sung to and this is a great time to start. Also, consider the lyrics of what you pick. Do they represent things about you? Making this slight change in what you listen to will also make another shift. You will feel better. This powerful source can take you quickly from a stressed perspective to one of gaiety very quickly.

Contact from your baby

In this trimester you will experience the exciting moment when you feel your baby inside of you. It's an odd sensation, but unexplainably phenomenal. It's when the connection you've been offering to your baby is really reciprocated. You've put yourself out there, you've yelled from the rooftops, "Hey, I'm your mom!" But now, now you have someone saying, "Hey, I'm here. I'm your child!" I always found this very exciting.

It's also an interesting way of getting to know your baby better. All three of our children have used their movements differently. Our first daughter would play with me. She would play, play, play all the time. I would tap on one spot and she would meet me there, then I would tap another and she would move to it. I spent ages tapping away. Our second daughter would use it as communication, especially if she didn't like something; then I would get a good kick. Then I used it as a communication step with our son. Because I decided not to seek medical advice until much later in the pregnancy, I asked our baby to start kicking and moving as soon as possible so that I could know he was alright. He started very early on, and then it was pretty regular. Whenever I noticed I hadn't felt anything for a bit and got a bit worried, he'd sense it and give me a good wallop. I may have felt black and blue by the ninth month but I could never be mad about it, for it told me that not only was he healthy and strong, but we had a great connection already.

It was the second trimester that I started to play with getting to know our baby. Find out who your tenant is. This was when I started to get a sense of who it was and what sex it had taken form in. This leads to one of my favourite exercises.

Exercise One

Sit in a quiet space and close your eyes. Shift your focus to your breath and let it drop down to where your bump sits. Watch as your bump rises slightly.

Slowly, let yourself start to imagine your child. Not in images of what they will look like, but rather who it is. This will be subtle and might take awhile, but slowly you will get the essence of the person. It's a bit like when suddenly someone is standing behind you and you know who it is. The baby's energy will start to pour over you and you will know them at your core. Your spirit will meet its spirit and you will bond.

Don't have any pressure if you don't feel this right away. Make a verbal request, say out loud, "I'm so curious about who you are, I would love to get to know you now."

It might not come at that moment, but one day you might be taking out the rubbish or in the shower, and you will get the feeling of not being alone. Then acknowledge it and say out loud, "Oh, there you are. Hi."

It feels so good when you cross that barrier of seeing this thing growing inside of you (making you tired, making you constipated, making you hormonal) as a person, as some other soul, as someone to share your road of life with. This is not going to be a doll. It's not a robot. Already this little person is forming ideas, and reactions, already it reads energy through what it hears and feels. What an amazing thing! Also, it will help you through those tough days, when you're faced with a cranky or upset baby, to recall that essence and see him for Who He Really Is. It is easy to fall into the trap of seeing your baby as

Who They Really Are

"The Baby," but comfort and understanding will come faster and more naturally if you see him as himself.

Exercise Two

I can't stress more how much fun it is to get to know your baby at this time. Take up your note book and write letters to your baby. Even if its in journal form and full of news of your day, make notes about its movements and what you are thinking about it all. Not only does this let you know how you will relate to your child even when its all grown up (and yes, it will grow up) it provides you with a great memento and a resource on those stressful days about what its all about. Do it now, before you feel it falls down on the priority list and while you have time and silence to think.

Exercise Three

If you have any garden space at all, consider planting a vegetable garden for you and your baby. If you are planning to breastfeed, then you are creating the best food to be past on through you. And even if you aren't nursing, it means that when your baby is over four months old, you can start to feed it directly from your garden. Start to plan this out now and put the love of your baby directly into your work. Consider carrots, squashes, sweet potatoes, peas, green beans, anything simple that you will be able to cook and make fresh food out of. It is an amazing experience and a concrete step in the direction of getting ready to care for your baby on many levels. Also, it is a wonderful analogy to taking part in nature and how everything works together. After all, not to sound too poetic, but currently, you are the garden.

Exercise Four

Place your hands on your ever-growing belly, and let them rise up and down with your breathing. Then imagine the feeling of wellbeing flowing through you and through your hands to your baby. Let this become like the sensation of a hug, the exchange of love and comfort between the two of you. You will find yourself doing naturally this through the day, even in precautionary ways like not letting your bump get bumped by anything or anyone, or even placing your hands against your bump when around people you don't mix well with. However, take this time to really sit and enjoy it. You may feel your baby come to meet your hands, which you can feel as the hug reciprocated. As the weeks progress, you will take this exercise into your daily life, and a friendly hand on your stomach, even during conversations, can serve as a gentle reminder to you and your baby that you are connected, doing well, there for each other, comforting each other and loving each other in that moment.

Often people will decide that they too want to touch your stomach to see if the baby will kick. Unless it was my husband, I have never had a baby who liked this and quite frankly the request to kick has never been fulfilled except for me. I've always felt uncomfortable with other people's asking. It's as if some energy barrier is crossed and invades the baby's space. But like with all things in this book, follow your spirit. If it feels *off* to you, make some excuse, or simply say, "I'd rather you didn't. There'll be plenty of time after he's born." If you feel okay with it, let it happen, but stay connected to your baby. If you feel it shy away, put off the touching. Then again, you might have a little socialite, who can't wait to interact with other people and this is its idea of perfect connection to Source. Not that I suggest getting anyone and everyone to touch your stomach in that case, but you know what I mean.

Note - These exercises are applicable for the third trimester as well. Which means to say, keep doing them and exploring you and your baby through them; it's an ongoing experience. There's no getting it done and no getting it wrong; just have a fun time with it all.

Feeling Good under the scrutinizing eyes of the medical system

I think this is a good time to talk about the medical profession. During my first pregnancy, I was committed to it, my second I had a bad experience with it, and my third I tiptoed into it, and ended up having our son at home. He was healthy and Swine Flu was around the hospitals, so I phoned them up and told them to forget about us; we had him checked out by a GP. Yes, I'm probably a doctor's worst nightmare, but I won't ever tell a woman not to see one. I will, however, tell them to use them and not see them as God.

You and your baby are connected. You will know if something is wrong and when all is right. Chances are the effect of stress and worry often given to you by fear-based people can cause you to think about those opinions all day long, and those thoughts would then affect your cells, which means things won't go well. See where I'm going with this. However, don't go putting a happy face on the situation while really underneath you are terrified. That is important info. That is what your basement is, so clean it up first.

So, my opinion is this. This is what I did, and this is how I put myself in a comfort zone.

Eat well. Sure there are people out there that have healthy babies while living on fast foods. But you know you'll have a bit of a "I shouldn't be doing this." Also, you'll get constipated and piles, and that is a stress in itself. Include living foods in your diet, lots and lots of green leafy vegetables. Lots of fruit. The life giving properties of these foods are remarkable, and what a lovely feeling it is, to be eating directly from nature in order to feed your unborn child. Eat plenty of whole grains, and enjoy your food. There is nothing more joy-giving than a good plate in front of you, so eat well and live well. (And don't listen to anyone who tells you about gaining weight. If you are eating well, it will be all baby. Also, tell them that more complications arise from underweight births.)

Before anyone checks your blood pressure, breathe a few times deeply and relax. I used to have to climb long stairways to get to my doctor, and I was always late. Then she wondered why I had such a high reading.

Eat a well-balanced meal before any blood tests. These pictures of your body are like photos of a certain time. There's no knowing if that's how your blood would have appeared the morning before, or after dinner tonight. The body is an amazing machine and knows how to fix any problems.

Testing often makes you look for problems, so only take tests when your instincts tell you too. Looking for problems makes you think about problems. Thinking about problems, well, that makes problems.

For this same reason, watch what pregnancy books you read. Some of the most popular are the most fear based. Drop them quickly and run. Some of my favourites are: Dr. Robert S. Mendelsohn's <u>How to Have a Healthy Child in Spite of Your Doctor</u>, and Deepak Chopra's <u>Magical Beginnings</u> and for a bit more information than inspiration I suggest every parent reads Jennifer Margulis' <u>Your Baby, Your Way.</u>

Watch yourself. Stay grounded whenever you approach a check up. Remember, your body knows how to do this. If you have been watching what you put into your body, and feel good about how you've eaten, if you have been watching your thoughts and feel good about where you are, you are in the optimum place to have a healthy pregnancy and a happy, healthy baby. And if any doctor tries to put fear into you, or tells you about all the things that can go wrong, it's better to intervene before it does; get another doctor.

Learn and feel. That is my approach. If anyone tells you something is happening that's unusual, before you do anything about it, research about four sources on it. If you hear something that sounds worrisome, ask, read, find out. Look into yourself and how you feel about how it is going. If all feels well, refuse treatments. If it feels Off, research and go the course that feels right to you.

And if any medical professional says I am wrong, it's not me I'm telling you to listen to. I'm saying listen to your inner guidance system, your spirit, your soul, your God, first. Listen to your baby second, and then listen to anyone else… provided they don't disagree with the first two!

Affirmation

Hello, Little One. I am so glad to meet you. I am so excited to have you in my life. We will have great fun you and I. Together let us take part in the magic that surrounds us. I give you my love. I give you my heart. Even though we haven't seen each other yet, know that I am here. I am aware of you. We are connected, and no matter what, always will be. I love you.

A guide to being a spiritually aware parent

Chapter Four

Third Trimester

Ah, the last one. The first month of the third trimester can seem like delivery is right around the corner. Suddenly, you have people giving you showers or rushing around to go shopping with you. Sorting out baby clothes, cribs, car seats, birth plans, as well as feeling heavier and heavier makes you jump into a "should do" place, which really takes the glory out of where you are.

Slow down. You still have three months, and for every child I've had, I've gotten ready way, way too early; there's time after the baby comes. Your partner or family members will be happy to pick up any forgotten items. So relax. No baby is going to wear every onesie, every sleeper, and use every receiving blanket within the first few days of life. They won't even notice if they wear the same one twice.

So, keep connected, now more than ever before. Take time whenever you can to stop and talk to your baby. Rest your reassuring hands on your bump and tell that spirit embodied inside of you, that everything is going to be okay. Its space might be getting more cramped, it might be moving differently, but soon it will have all the space in the world to stretch out. Remember this, especially if you are continually being kicked or punched. This is not an outward attack on you. Your baby is in no means intentionally lashing out. Rather, they want to move and there's very little room. You're not the only one who might be scared.

Labor and delivery

The world and popular media has made birth into a horror story. Movies are filled with women on the brink of death, screaming in agony. (Have you ever noticed that they are always on their backs, which is not a position your instincts will suggest?) Every women you know has some horror story, some scar, some stretch mark to tell you about. However, you can make your experience different. After all, you know different. And yes, there are women without the horror, the scar and the stretch marks, me for example. There are plenty like me. It's just that people don't spread those stories. They like the juicy gossip sessions to satisfy their addiction to friction. I suggest you try to be the story no one talks about.

You have been staying connected to You, to your Source and to your baby. You know that within you, every cell in your body is working day and night to fulfill its function. Your body has been waiting for this moment. Not for just the last six months, but rather for your whole life. Your body has every hormone, muscle and blood cell it takes to make a baby and deliver it safely into your arms. All you have to do is breathe and allow it all to take place.

In this last trimester, it is important to get to know the process of labour and delivery. Watch yourself as you learn about this. If a feeling of fear comes up, don't push it aside, and don't let it overtake you. Rather look at it squarely, and remind yourself of this next paragraph.

"Most complications and difficulties in women's birthing experiences come from a lack of trust in their own bodies. However, I know my body was made to do this. My body will find this process as easy as taking its next breath, only I will notice it more as it involves muscles I've never used. Most women are taught to resist this experience. Many women don't understand the power of staying connected both to the baby they carry and to the Source from which we all come from. Science uses the common denominator to base studies on; however, I do not live as others. I am not a common denominator but a deliberate creator of my experience and these studies do not apply to me."

Is there part of this paragraph that doesn't ring true to you? Are you ready to call yourself a deliberate creator of your experience when it comes to the delivery of your baby?

Remember, the Law of Attraction is based on what you feel. You can't sit in your room, meditating on the words, "Good birth. Good birth. No pain. No pain." That mantra would stir up a feeling place that rings of, "Mayday! Mayday! Gonna hurt. Gonna hurt."

Who They Really Are

Words, descriptions, details, it's all unnecessary. Rather, you have a foundational job to do for this to all go well. Focus on the things that are going well, relax and trust in your body and imagine how you want the birth to go. Practice well and practice it often and you may well have the best birthing experience ever recorded.

This could probably be in the exercise list; however, it is more of a mantra, so we'll call it a thought processes instead. Make this your pattern of thought, not in a set time of day, but in every spare moment. Not just in every spare moment, but when walking to the car, getting the laundry, picking up the phone. The thought is simply this:

Collect in your mind things that make you feel good, whatever that may be. Perhaps you get a thrill rushing up and down your spine when you imagine holding your baby in your arms for the first time. We'll look at this first.

Thought Process One

Feel the excitement as the little bundle is past to you. They are healthy, and happy to finally be with you. See its tiny little fingers as they wrap around yours for the first time. Count its toes. There are five on each foot. Imagine the sensation of feeding this little being for the first time, as you lead it gently to your breast. Feel your partner over your shoulder gazing in wonder at what the two of you have brought into the world.

If you have certain conditions you hope to experience at this time, add those in too. But don't let them throw you out of the feeling place of your image. For instance, you might want your birthing room to be quiet, as this miracle takes place. You might want the doctors or attendants to be kind, listening and not very busy. You might want everyone to be cheerful. Add all this on a feeling place, not words or thoughts. For example, a quiet place would make you feel relaxed, while friendly and stress-free staff would make you feel safe and uplifted. As you paint this scene, repeat it often if it makes you feel good.

If you still shudder at the idea your upcoming delivery or if you start to lose the feeling of your dream birth then try the next exercise on for size.

Thought Process Two

Pick something that makes you feel so wonderful that you could burst. This could be a hike to a mountaintop, lying on a beach in a bikini, sitting with a loved one on a sofa watching a movie, a bubble bath or a slow boat to China. Whatever makes you feel so good that when you think about it, you get excited even though you aren't there now. Yes, this is the power of imagination and yes it works. Sink into the idea that you feel good in; live in it, take in the smells, the feels, the tastes, whatever brings you joy. Then revisit it again and again. If it loses its joy-giving factor, pick another one. Fill your life over the next three months with thoughts that make you jive with joy. If you one day can't think of one, use the magic key of appreciation and fill your day with loving things in your life now.

Who They Really Are

It sounds simple and probably illogical. But it is clinically proven that stress and fear is a huge factor in birth complications. It is also scientifically proven that your thoughts affect your stress levels. On a spiritual level, we've talked about the Law of Attraction being attracted to how you feel. Well, your thoughts are keys to how you feel, and what you think can literally change every experience. And the way I see it is that if thinking of things that make you feel good, and letting that feeling flow over you makes you feel better, and feeling wonderful keeps your baby feeling closer to everything You Both Really Are, then really... can anything bad ever come out of that?

There's no limit to how long to do this for, no set meditation standard, no 3-4 times daily stuff, just whenever and however often you can. I will tell you, though, that it takes 17 seconds of holding a thought without contradicting it, (for example a contradicting thought would be "I would love to be lying on the beach in my bikini, not that I will ever fit in a bikini again,") 17 seconds of uncontradicted thought to change your feeling place. After 17 seconds another thought will join on to strengthen your feeling of it, and then another. In fact, it is said that it only takes 68 seconds of uncontradicted thought to change the course of the Law of Attraction. So really, even if you haven't even thought of spiritual practices before this point in pregnancy, you don't have to beat yourself up that you are attracting a bad experience. Just sit and consciously focus your emotions, your feelings and your thoughts to something that feels good. Let Source take care of the rest.

If you are feeling extra stressed, worried or just off, take care of your emotional state by watching a funny movie, or getting outside and appreciating everything you see. Love, Love,

Love and Laugh. That will immediately set the wheels in motion for an easy, beautiful and happy birthing experience.

The power of energy

I want to pass on a bit of information to you that I learnt after my baby experience, but I wish I'd known then what I know now. I had the chance to study the energy healing process of Therapeutic Touch, which is similar to Reiki yet accepted in the medical community as it has been studied and practiced by nurses. Therapeutic touch acknowledges that we are made of energy, that energy literally flows though us and all around us. We emit it. When we are stressed or as daily niggles wear on us, we can create blocks of energy which stops the flow within us.

Now, imagine for a moment energy flowing in from the top of your head, it flows in and through to the soles of your feet. The more flow through to the ground, the more flow is created with energy pouring in from above. Hence the feeling of being grounded when connected to our Source, the energy is flowing freely. If we feel headachy, or are over thinking, or sometimes we feel stressed in our stomach and have problems breathing deeply, we can feel our energy flow being held back and the flow can't be created.

Therapeutic Touch is a three level course which passes on techniques to use energy to relieve pain in others and create flow, but there are a few things that I feel you can practice right away, and are incredibly empowering for you, for your unborn baby and for your baby once they arrive. It's an exciting and liberating thing to integrate into your daily life.

First, "Where attention goes, energy flows." If you feel ungrounded, stressed, nervous or simply put, disconnected; put focus on your feet. Rotate your ankles, wiggle your toes, massage them, better yet ask your partner to massage them. Have a foot bath or simply imagine roots growing out from underneath the soles of your feet. Soon your body with tingle with the increased energy flow. When you think of it, if we have a headache, we think about the pain in our head and it grows worse. When we train ourselves to draw the energy away from the head by focusing on the feet, it melts away. Try it, it works.

Second, with the palms of your hands faced together but not touching, practice making an energy ball. You will feel slight resistance as you play with the space between your two hands. When you feel the resistance, imagine it as a ball letting it grow within that space. This can become quite mesmerizing to begin with and as you practice you will get use to the feeling of an energy field.

Now, practice finding it on others and other things. Feel it on your own legs (If you do it on yourself or on anyone else always practice in sweeping movements downwards, from head to foot, remember the flow of energy) practice on plants, on pets (dogs love it… cats think you're crazy, but what's new!) sense the energy on all things, and then back to your feet. Always end energy work back to your feet; hold them, ground them.

You can play with this as you practice. Send love and healing to those you love, send it to your baby. Feel the presence of living positive energy around and emitting from everyone.

This sudden awareness for energy will help in these later days of pregnancy and with the practice of the awareness it will help in labor. Practice the flow of your energy and you practice aligning to what your source and your body know already.

Contemplating Breastfeeding

It goes without saying that the spiritual bonding of breastfeeding is unmatched. Although the father that gets to feed the bottle-fed baby might argue that point. I am an avid breastfeeding advocate. I won't discredit the amazing bond it forms and I'll happily pump if someone else wants the bonding experience. When I first wrote this book I was expecting to wean my son after he was about 18 months. What followed, which we'll look more at in weaning, was a five year journey together. It had its ups and downs, but as I look back I know that it was by all means the best thing for him. It provided him with a sense of balance in an unbalanced time and an empowerment to me to help him at times when nothing else would.

First, let's take it from your baby's perspective. As pure positive energy coming into human form, over the past months it has gotten used to being provided for. Remember we talked about the placenta being the Universal Manager? Suddenly, your baby will have the jolting experience of breathing air, a large space, and the feeling of touch. When it is passed to your arms, it will have a sense of where it has come from, and when it is fed from your breasts it will have a reassuring glimpse of the feeling of being provided for by the Universal Manager. You will become that security. I shudder at the thought of me being rushed to the nursery and bottle fed by strangers when I was born. I must have been an emotional wreck, and quite frankly my mother will tell you I screamed my head off most of my infancy to prove it.

This security for your baby will continue well into infancy and for as long as you breastfeed. Your instincts will stay in tune with your child and you will be able to know the right time to quit by their cue; feedings start to naturally deplete as your child starts to eat more and more solid food.

Also, as a spiritual benefit, it is so less stressful. I fell into the pressure to bottle feed with our first daughter, and my god, you are so tied down. Schedules are prominent, and you can't overfeed. You find yourself rushing to make a bottle with a screaming baby in your arms. I was always in a panic. With breastfeeding, you can control the atmosphere. You can still schedule, but it will be again from your baby's cues. You will notice their patterns and follow them naturally.

As I describe these things, I hope you watch yourself. As I write them, I notice myself getting stressed and feeling off on one side, but as I write about doing things by instinct, following nature's cues and trusting in it all, I feel so much better. Is it the same for you?

Now, if you don't want to breastfeed, simply put, don't. Do nothing that would breed resentment or hostility within you. Do nothing that you would see as a chore and a pain in the neck. That would do so much more harm to you and your baby than any of the benefits of breastfeeding could outweigh.

Again, as with all things in your life, this is *your* experience. Design it intentionally. But try out different things, test them out and how they feel. You are creating an experience for two.

Exercise One

As people talk to you about labour and delivery, listen for the suggestions of visualization. This does actually work, as it relaxes your muscles and tells your body you are allowing it to do its job. Don't be afraid to practice this now. It won't bring on early labour. So practice an image that feels good to you. Practice it so that when needed, you can pull it out and relax into it, to really let all your cells know you are present and in a state of allowing. Often, people will suggest the image of a flower opening up. This is a great one, as it's gentle, natural and relaxing. It is also what is happening on a physical scale. So design your flower to focus on. What kind is it? Colour? How close can you see it? This image can become quite important to you if you like it, and its nice to have in the back pocket of your mind to pull you back from getting stressed or worried when your time comes.

If you don't feel connected to a flower image, don't worry. There are no "shoulds" here. Rather, look back at the thoughts that have made you feel good. Are there images in there that are easy for you to pull up at anytime? Practice them for the 17-second exercise. Pick one or two of them and practice them for a few days. Do they make you feel relaxed and in a state of well being? That will do perfectly. It is your feeling here as always, not the fact that the flower opens.

Exercise Two

Get crafty. Make something for your baby if you sew, or even if you don't and want to. This can be as simple as small burp cloths, which can be useful. Take some soft cloth and sew a thicker material like towel to the back, then consider embroidering a small image on a corner. Make sure any loose threads aren't sticking out that could choke your baby or get stuck in his little fingers or mouth. If you feel more courageous, make a small toy or blanket, even if it's on display for the first while.

Exercise Three

Make an Inspiration Board for yourself. Cut out pictures that make you feel good, images of places or people that make you jive. Print out quotes or sayings that immediately raise your feeling or mood. Write words or find pictures of simple things you appreciate. Even take some photos of things around you that make you feel good. Paste them on a piece of hardboard and hang it somewhere you will see it often. If you don't want to go to all this effort, then simply make a box full of this type of stuff. Fill it with good feeling things. Have fun with this and know that even thinking about this stuff is putting you in a great place, a feeling good place and a place of connection to Source.

One last note as you head into your final stage. Still be at ease with all of this. You are not alone. Your baby has chosen you to experience as its portal. It has a definite intention and it wants to have as easy a time as you do. Trust that it has carved out for themselves a beautiful entrance into their life. Trust that you will do this together, that the bond you have formed already is so intertwined that both of you will understand what the other one needs.

Keep your connection, to your spirit, Your Source, and Your baby and expect the best of outcomes.

Affirmation

We are headed for a great adventure, dear one. I know that we are taken care of. We both have come from the same place and it is a place of well being. I trust that you are connected to that Source, I will be connected too. We were made to do this, and as one who approaches a fast running current on a raft, I approach your entrance into this world, with exhilaration, excitement, and expectation of only the best of outcomes. All will be well. I look forward to holding you close. I look forward to seeing you. I love you dearly.

Who They Really Are

A guide to being a spiritually aware parent

Part Two:
Infancy
and
Being the Great Provider

Who They Really Are

Special note for parents of special needs children

I would like to start off this chapter with something that will only affect a small percentage of parents.

If your baby has been born with any condition, such as Down syndrome or brain damage or even if it was born without life, you have to put yourself in a place of knowing there is no wrong. There are no mistakes. You have done your part in this process and your child has done theirs. This embodiment of pure, positive energy knew precisely how they wanted to experience the world, they mapped it out before arrival and, although you may feel surprised at their choice, you need not feel any guilt or bitterness at the result. There are no "problem" children. As someone who has first hand knowledge with both "Brain damaged" and "Down syndrome" children, I know the only mistake made was that they were labeled as such. They are as capable to feel and experience joy, love, happiness and elation as any human being and the bond with them can be just as powerful as it would have been if they had been born under the label "normal." Therefore, don't feel you suddenly are thrown into the world of "have tos" and learn how to deal with your child differently than you had anticipated. Avoid talking problem talk with anyone, and get quiet, still and into a place of feeling good yourself, so your instincts and connection can be the advice you need. If feeling good is too much to ask, simply feel well. Feel better. Find a thought that can simply take you out of any panic state and relax. Start a sentence with the words "At least" and find something to have appreciation for.

All is truly as it's supposed to be.

Special note for adoptive parents

So, perhaps the first section of this book wasn't relevant to you, as you are in the position of fulfilling one of the most wonderful experiences imaginable, that of an adoptive parent. Well, there's no reason that the following sections shouldn't pertain to you. However, a note specifically on this situation seems important.

First of all, congratulations! Even if your baby hasn't actually been born from your body, it doesn't diminish the bond you already have. This spirit chose you, perhaps not as its portal, but as who they would end up with. There was no miscalculation, no mistake. Rather, he only needed the contrast of being born to someone else (who probably offered them nine months of tortured emotion and upset) and now has the amazing bliss of being with someone who has chosen to love them completely. What a great vantage point for your child to start life. He will appreciate every kind word, hug and loving moment with you all the more.

Therefore, bask in your new life together, savor each moment and take the care to remember your baby's connection to everything he really is. If he has had a negative introduction to the world, make it you passion to show him the beauty of it. Love, love, love and breathe.

Who They Really Are

I have heard of adoptive parents who were riddled with guilt over not being able to breastfeed, or provide that little bit extra that nature provides. Pay no heed. Simply know that all is well, and you and your baby have previously arranged that you can provide *everything* he needs. You are a perfect match and the universe has made it so.

Through the following sections I do talk about nutrition during breastfeeding. Skip them if you wish, or scan them for ideas for the introduction of solids, which for bottle-fed babies can start around four months.

A guide to being a spiritually aware parent

Chapter 5

The First Month

Pure Positive Being in Human Form

<u>Bask in your Now</u>

Congratulations. There he is. Or she if the case may be. For the record, I will be referring to your baby as "*he*" for the rest of the book. Although most books now-a-days use the feminine article, it is more natural for me to use the male reference as right now our youngest is a boy. If you have had a girl, please imagine an "s" in front of the "h" to make "she."

There is nothing more awe-inspiring, more exhilarating, and more overwhelming than seeing that baby in your arms for

Who They Really Are

the first time. Pregnancy seems so far in the past suddenly and it seems a mystery as to how this small person got into your arms.

Savor these moments. People will be telling you to rest. Possibly, you'll have phone calls and visitors, but make sure you and your partner enjoy this new family member. This little bundle has finally arrived and he is with the people he has chosen to experience life with. Although you've been connecting for nine months, you finally have this little body in your arms; hug it, kiss it, and marvel at it. Let the magnitude of what has occurred sweep over you. Shower yourself with the love and satisfaction of where you are. You did it. You brought another living soul into this physical world and it will experience years and years of being a human because of you. On the flip side, this small being has enabled you to explore new ground, gain new experience, feel new emotions, and expand in love and understanding. I think it's time to thank each other. Revel in the knowledge that that expansion for both of you will continue for the rest of your lives.

Now, saying that, you are probably tired and sore. You are still the same person now that the baby is outside your body as you were when he was in. So, after feeding this small wonder for the first time and getting over the initial bewilderment, sleep when your baby sleeps. But before you drift off to slumber, take stock of your new vantage point.

There are few moments in life when we get to really stop and see ourselves in a new place in life. Life tends to progress like a rapid stream, and as the good stuff flows, usually we are just on for the ride. That exhilaration is great, but sometimes it feels like we missed something. That moment when your baby sleeps for the first time in your arms, when pregnancy and birth are behind you, and this glorious journey of parenthood is before you, is a specific pinnacle that I invite you to enjoy. You don't have to worry about creating a good experience right now, you don't have to worry about the future, and you don't even have to think about anyone else, just you and that small baby. Soak it up. If you have problems settling into what I mean, take stock of that little being in front of you.

Smell his hair, kiss his head, and let your finger caress his ears and his button nose. Count his fingers, see how the skin is really too big for them, let his hand wrap around a finger of yours and feel the thrill of that.

This is taking stock. This is getting to know the form of your child. The body you grew within you.

You have taken part in a miracle. Now, go to sleep and feel the wondrous being you are. Feel the power that has flowed through you, feel the magic you have taken part in, and feel as if you have just boarded a plane, safe and sound, for the greatest adventure of your life. Be satisfied that you have packed and prepared well. Now, take the first week and enjoy every minute you can.

Becoming your baby's Great Provider

"But he cries!" No, more than cries, he screams a scream that would cut glass. It's always a bit of a shock how much sound can come out of someone so small. Also, it's a shock to suddenly be woken up that way, to have to get used to jumping out of bed ready for action. Let's simplify this. No, I can't stop your baby from screaming, but let's see if a shift in perspective can take place.

Who They Really Are

Remember, this baby, although it might drive you crazy to hear it wail, is pure positive energy. It is connected and through your love and connective-ness, stays connected pretty much most of the time. There are three basic discomforts that are this baby's contrasts. You should actually appreciate this as this is one of the greatest parts of babies. It's simple. There are no hurt feelings, no scary dreams, no bad experiences being remembered the next day. Your baby's contrasts from its Source are simply:

1- Needs changing
2- Hunger
3- Colic, tummy ache or gas

I'm going to avoid talking about the first point. It doesn't take much to know when your baby needs changing. However, I will say: get into the habit of taking this time while he's on the changing table to connect and talk to him. Look into his eyes and smile. I am forever talking to my babies.

I know, what has this to do with Spiritual Parenting?

At this point, the way I see it is that your baby has just come from a place of pure positive energy. Before this moment, the placenta was its Great Provider, and now he's been thrust into the world and it seems so big. Suddenly these three contrasts have been thrust into his experience, and if they're not immediately taken care of, he can't do anything about them himself. That is frustration, that is upset, that is separation. Isn't that enough contrast for a little soul?

So whatever you do, don't get frustrated back, don't lash out, don't run out of the room saying I can't stand it. Not in these early days. Rather, ignore every person who has ever taught you to give hard love, or the phrase "cruel to be kind," and pick your baby up, hold him close and whisper, "It's okay." Then get rid of the three points of upset, and you'll be fine.

Avoiding hunger on breast milk

Why is it that no one talks about nutrition when breastfeeding? Oh, you might hear not to diet or to eat a few more calories. But what I've noticed, especially in the first few weeks is it is *nutrients* that fill a baby up with breast milk; nutrients and some starchy foods.

Potatoes have always been my breastfeeding best friend. Eat lots of them. This is a wonder food, as it's a complete food, and fills both you and your baby up. One of my favourite meals is simply mashed potatoes, peas and tuna with mayo. Also, roasted potatoes, baked potatoes with a filling for lunch, or even fried. Don't try to replace this with frozen fries, unless you really can't stand any more of them in their natural state.

My other lifesaver was hemp, which actually also stopped cradle cap within a day. Now, there's a lot of politics about this wonder-food, but its nonsense. It is a complete protein, plus complete EFAs. It makes breast milk! It comes in seeds, butter (being pressed seeds), milk (strained seeds) or oil. I've never liked the oil, but the butter replaces peanut butter in a shot, just get over it being green in colour. Green is good. The milk has a nutty taste, but is nice, and the seeds, also known as hemp hearts, are an amazing snack on the go.

The most important note on hemp is to make sure it's not rancid. DO NOT eat any that are kept in clear packaging. Rancid seeds and nuts aren't of any benefit at all, and can be harmful. Buy hemp in black or solid colour bags as this stops light from getting to them, which is the cause of rancidity. Also, store them in the fridge and return them to the fridge after each use. With those points in mind, have some hemp everyday and your baby will thrive on your milk.

Vegetables are a must. Leafy greens, peas, green beans, carrots, cabbage, try out whatever you can. Squash is a nice filler too; however, watch how it affects your baby. Lentils are a great protein giver, but watch out for a bad effect on the baby if you aren't use to them or if you haven't had them during pregnancy.

Enjoy snack foods too, and don't go to bed hungry, even if you just grab a slice of toast. Your baby will be eating at night too.

Tell your partner that even though he can't bottle feed the baby he can still provide food for it. In the first week when you are still off your feet, ask him to feed you. Go natural, go with nutrients in mind, with all the vitamins, minerals and health you can muster. Don't decide to limit yourself now, with a barrage against wheat or anything else unless you have a definite allergy. Enjoy your food, chew it well, and trust that your body is sending all that good stuff straight to your milk supply for the next feeding.

Don't fall into the trap that you have to set a routine up. Breastfeeding at first seems endless, that you are always doing it, but it will regulate itself just fine as your baby fills out and becomes less hungry. These first few weeks are just a way of stabilizing your child, and getting it into a comfortable place so in a few weeks he can start to look around at the beautiful world he now lives in. Trust that this time is a brief one, and provide for your baby as the Great Provider.

One other thing to remember about breast milk (sorry bottle-feeding mothers for going on about this): if down the line your baby gets sick, such as a cold or flu, it can be used through nutrition to fight off any germs. Eat lots of carrots to boost your baby's immunity and fight any lung congestion, eat apples and fresh fruit for extra nutrients, and garlic, which is a natural antibiotic. Your body will give the correct amount of everything to your baby and you will feel like you are truly helping your child, not being left in the frustrating position of just tending a sick person.

Colic, first pain, first contrasting experience

The medical and scientific world will still tell you that the cause of colic in an infant is a mystery. Some blame gas caused by air that has gotten trapped in your infant's stomach that then gives him tummy cramps and a lot of pain. Some suggest that under-developed digestive systems can lead to colic, and some suggest diet. None can explain why it always happens around the same time of day and none of it helps the distress it causes the baby, parents and the home itself.

Whatever the cause though, it is very common for a newborn to cry uncontrollably for a couple of hours. It usually occurs at the same time of the day, often around 6-7 pm, but sometimes in the middle of the night. It can be truly overwhelming for a new parent to see their bundle of joy turn into a miserable, screaming baby.

Now, as a parent wanting to come from a spiritual place of wellbeing and joy, how do you cope with such a situation? Naturally, the event is going to fill you with stress. After the first few days, you will start to feel frustrated and anxious. Worry and concern will kick in and the idea that this is how parenthood will always be will fill you with terror. The fact that your sleep is limited and you could bump into walls for tiredness doesn't help either. You might read or be told that studies have shown that stress can be another cause of colic, as the baby picks up on the stress and concern of the parent and reacts to it. Funny how being told stress causes problems can make us more stressed not to be stressed.

Well, let's try to change perspective on this, shall we?

First, it's important to understand what your baby is going through. To see the situation from his perspective will tell you more what he needs. It will also stop him from turning into a thing for you. An annoying thing that screams and takes all your time, rather than the true bundle of loveliness you know he is.

Nine months ago your baby was only Pure, Positive Spirit. As a spiritual parent, you are aware that all of us are more than these physical bodies. Call it our Soul, our Spirit, or higher self, it is all a source of pure, positive divinity. This is what your baby was and through pregnancy your baby became physical. However, its physical experience in your womb was limited and without much negative experience. It was never hungry or tired. Rather, it lived taken care of entirely. Now, he has been born; the wait time is longer for these needs to be met. This transition can be harder for some babies than for others. The introduction to stress, be it from parents or others around him, is also a huge contrast to where they've come from as negative emotions don't exist on a soul level.

So what does this mean on a practical basis for you, the fed up, frustrated and tired parent? It means opportunity. It means being forced to put aside your usual day-to-day life for the time of your baby's transition, which is indicated by bouts of colic. It is time to be as soul-full as you really can be. It's not a question of adding meditation times or church to your already overwhelming schedule. Rather, it is through finding things that bring you joy and relief. It is taking care of your thoughts and allowing yourself to let go of tension, stress and a sense of trying to keep life under control.

Therefore, when your baby isn't colicky, appreciate it. Love your darling bundle, hold him, hug him, memorize him. Try to get a sense of Who he is and Who he will grow up to be. Appreciate the world around you, the world that soon your baby will be able to enjoy. Love, love, love and breathe.

Relax and remember, your baby is in transition, but so are you. You don't have to be getting it all right. See your baby as adapting to new surroundings and try to remember a time when you had to do so too.

When a colic spasm starts, don't panic. Breathe and relax and rest in the fact that you will be holding your baby and unable to do anything else. Don't try to get anything else done and struggle against it. Change the scene and distract both yourself and your baby. Take a walk, go outside, put on nice music and dance about. Even though he's young, show him things around you, sing to him, and stimulate him.

This is a good time to remember your energy work we discussed earlier. If your baby is feeling distressed and those legs are crunching up, help him relax with helping his energy flow. Massage his feet with one hand while holding him with your other arm, trace your fingers down his back, even simply hold the process of shifting his energy downwards in your mind, and your energy field will help his. Intention is everything in the field of energy.

Promise yourself that this time will be one of joy not stress, of Spirit not aggravated separation.

Ironically, the more you look at these times as a time for spirit, the faster colic will disappear from your life. Another indicator that your energy is affecting your baby's. Trust me. Soon, you won't even remember the fact that your baby ever had it.

Exercise One

Before you go to sleep and in the first moment you wake up, let the feeling of appreciation flood your soul. If your baby is in your arms, and if you are in that loving state, feel appreciation for the fact your baby chose you. If you are missing parts of your pre-parenting life, love something outside of your child. Love your bed, your pillow, love your home, your yard. Don't feel guilty if you aren't brought to a state of joy with the thought of your child. That's okay, and after a rough night, it is sometimes too much to ask from anyone. Rather, make yourself feel good with a blissful feeling. This will make you a more responsive parent faster than trying to force feeling good about your baby. Other moments that it's possible to reach for better feeling thoughts are during feedings, and changing time, also when you are in the bath or shower. Make a list of things you love, that make you feel good. Images that you can create a feeling for, such as a beach at sunset, or a hot summer's day, can transport you to a different feeling place if you practice them.

Exercise Two

If you made an inspiration board when you were pregnant, now is the time to use. If you gathered good feeling things in a box, consider pasting them up somewhere now so you can see them often. Have fun in the land of your thoughts. You will feel good and your baby will sense that mom is happy.

A baby's world is circular without its knowledge. If you feel good, your baby responds to it and feels good, and if baby feels good, you feel better. If you are stressed, your baby senses it and gets upset, then you get more stressed and the baby freaks out more. Break this cycle by feeling the best you can. If your thoughts don't enter at a focused point, relax. Watch a funny movie, or listen to some fun and mood raising music. Love your feeling place no matter what.

Now, this may sound like selfishness now that someone else is depending on you, but you don't have to feel good at the expense of another. If your baby is crying don't tell him he has to shut up so you can find a good feeling place. You won't feel good with your aggravation towards your new loved one, so you won't get where you want to be anyway. Rather, put your baby in a carrier or stroller and get some fresh air. Feed him, or change him, holding yourself in a bit of suspension. Let feeling good flow in, or know it is flowing in soon.

Simply put, relax into this. No one is expecting you to reach any goal, to become super mom overnight or to find this all easy. Feel good in the moments. Love, love, love and breathe.

Who They Really Are

Affirmation

Dear One, I love you. I know that this physical apparatus is not the complete you. I know that sometimes the discomforts of physical life can be confusing and upsetting for you and hard to get used to. We are getting used to our new vantage points together. I know it will be alright. I love you and will help you get used to your new surroundings. Let us embrace this new world together. With each pain, desire, or upset I will be there for you. I will try to make it pass quickly. I hope you know how committed I am to making your transition a good one. However, this is new to me too. I sometimes might get overwhelmed and that's alright. Let us keep the connection we made while pregnant. Together, let us feel good.

Special note about partners and co-parenting

It may seem that the focus of this book is mothers, but I would like to think that a partner could benefit as equally from the information provided.

A father can be as spiritually aware of their child's spiritual connection as a mother. After all, this child has chosen *both* his parents and the situation he was born into as the optimal experience to start life. Therefore, whether in a co-parenting situation or a single parent one, a parent can relax and know that everything is just as it is meant to be.

Fathers, breathe and relax with all of this. Know that the connection is there and you will sense his needs, wants, and connection to Who He Really Is as strongly as his mother will. Talk to your baby, sing and play with him to a point of connection. Make him laugh.

The relationship between a father and his child can be one of the most beautiful things imaginable, as a baby will often feel he can spread his wings a little bit more with a father. With his mother he tends to be more coddled; with a father he can play, laugh, and be comforted at the same time as exploring his own true nature. Often a relationship is changed by the arrival of a new family member. Disagreements about the best route to take on major decisions can have partners disconnecting from their own true selves and from each other for what they think is the benefit of their offspring. The truth is, nothing can be of benefit to your child if it doesn't come from a place of connection to all you really are. You have to feel good first, get connected first and then let the answers flow to you.

Who They Really Are

Breastfeeding, co-sleeping, whether to let a child cry it out, or how to discipline are all foundational decisions that affect both parents as well as their baby. No matter what, each member of the whole family has to find a way to return to a good feeling position before deciding what course to take.

It seems to me that in these foundational stages, communication is key. A father should never be put in the position of having to do something that feels *off* to him, on the basis that it's what the mother says feels good to her. Therefore, before discussing any issues, both parents should take some time, either apart or together, to feel good. They should then do something that reaffirms Who They Are together. Romantic dinners, starlit walks, making love or gazing into each others eyes reminds yourselves of the connection you have, which was the basis of your child choosing you in the first place.

Be honest with your partner and yourself and listen to each other. If say, co-sleeping feels right to one of you and *off* to the other, say so and then look for a happy common ground. Having a baby in the bed with you might worry one of you, so look at co-sleeping units, which allow a baby to sleep with you while in their own protected space. If one of you likes to have bed as your own space, agree to have your baby sleep in his crib until he wakes up in the middle of the night. When you both parent from a place of feeling good, then you will find the answers naturally present themselves as you work in the same direction.

Play off each other and trust each other's connection. Who's feeling the best? Who's connected at the moment and in a state of feeling good? Is one of you coming from a state of worry or fear? Then go with the other's opinion. Every person on this planet moves between being connected and disconnected; it's what makes us human and makes us grow and expand. Therefore, with two people acting from a place of spiritual awareness, chances are your child will have at least one connected parent most of the time. Anyway, there's no harm in trying out one partner's idea and seeing how it feels. Just respect each other's feeling spaces and see if it feels off after trying it.

Having a child can help a relationship grow deeper and stronger. If you keep your connection to Source and everything your really are, then connect to everything your partner really is, together you can help your child connect and together will instinctually know the course to take. You are an example to your child, how you speak together, how you feel together, how you smile to each other all give foundational perspectives to your baby. It will be their default of how they view love, life and home.

In the long run, your child will one day grow and start a life of their own. One day you will turn around and only see each other again.

Therefore, it is vital to relax into a state of feeling good together and not to stress if you feel it's not "going your way." If you feel *off* about something, say so and allow the situation to make you expand and catch up. Sometimes by just letting go of pushing against what you don't want, by trusting Source, feeling good and focusing on the positive, suddenly your partner will come up with the same solution you were hoping for.

By empowering each other, you empower your home and create a space for your child to feel empowered in too.

Who They Really Are

A guide to being a spiritually aware parent

Chapter 6

Second to Sixth month

Being the Great Provider

Ah, things are getting easier. Or at least they seem to be becoming a little more natural. By the second month you are forming new habits and it is easier to feel at ease with it all.

What's happening in your baby's world

Your new baby is starting to wake up a bit to the world around him. His eyes can focus more and you even start getting glimpses of a smile here and there. He has arrived in his body to the fullest and with that comes a new awareness to his surroundings. Jump on board with this and have some fun. Your voice has always been an important part of you for your baby since it was the part of you he knew first, but suddenly your eye contact, your smile and your expression become equally important. This is when you can start to play with your baby a bit, just through a song, a sound or even just chatter.

What does your baby think? He is fascinated! Everything is new to his eyes. Every sunray, every snowflake, every feel of a blanket. I remember our eldest daughter used to have this wool blanket that was edged with satin ribbon. I used to come into her room and find her just lying there feeling the edge with a look of awe on her face. Our son has always been amazed by his hands and feet. I still find him trying to get a foot to his mouth.

With your baby's new wonderment with life comes a different set of contrasts, but the first three (changing, hunger, tummy ache or gas) still apply. The additions are only to be watched for and can come on more from a feeling of unfamiliarity or uneasiness.

Behaviour

Around the second month you might find your baby doesn't like to be held by other people. He might feel strange even when new people are in the room. Some people call this playing shy, but really it's a sense of insecurity. Your baby probably still remembers the common voices that he heard around you during pregnancy, and those still feel like security to him. However, people that sound less familiar, or maybe make you feel less like yourself, will make him feel the contrast of uneasiness. It's totally natural, and it soon passes if you simply hold your baby and comfort him. Then, while holding him, talk to the person and let your baby knows you are okay. Remembering the concept of energy fields again, other people "feel different" energetically, and it takes getting use to. If he doesn't want to be held by anyone but you, that's okay, unless it frustrates you or you have to do something. Then pass him on to someone he is used to having around or at least hearing around, and let them try to bond. If it fails, do what you need to do fast and then return for a reassuring hug and close the gap that was momentarily created.

You might also see signs of first fears, especially as teething kicks in. Sometimes it might feel you aren't even allowed to go to the bathroom alone without your baby flipping out on you. Be easy on this early separation anxiety. You might feel inclined to say, "He has to get used to it," and leave him crying, but honestly, as Spirit, he wants to know you're not far. So, let him be near you. If you go to the bathroom, talk to him from the other room; if you go other places, hold him. When our youngest started teething at around four months, he would freak whenever I put him in his bed. For one week I let him sleep in my arms while I worked. By the next week, he was comfortable being moved to the couch beside me while I worked, and by two weeks after that he felt secure in his bed again, although he was always in co-sleeping with us by the time we went to bed. Don't think any of this time is forever, as it will literally be moment to moment for things to change. Knowing that, go with the flow and follow your baby's instincts and your own.

This same reaction can happen when you take your baby out somewhere. If you are in the habit of rushing out and getting your chores done, then this pace will unsettle your baby. You might get an hour or two, pace it right after a feed so he can comfortably sleep, but try to keep your stress level low. Keep feeling good yourself so your baby will sense your connection and know it is all alright. Building on the circular idea of a baby's world, he is now getting worried about you. If you are stressed, then he picks up on that and feels unstable. "What's up with mom?" becomes the concern, which will spiral into a fit of tears. This isn't pressure to not feel stress; rather, breathe and note how you are feeling in each situation. If you feel stressed, don't try to do everything in one outing. Breathe deeply, feel good, and focus on just a few priorities.

Now, if you were supposed to meet someone or do something you were really looking forward to, don't feel you have to be trapped at home and miss it. Rather, pull over, feed your baby, make him comfortable, get yourself connected and then go to what you are looking forward to. Chances are you will feel good there, and your baby will see that. In that security, he'll probably sleep or be truly entertaining for the people around you.

Routine

It seems to me that there are usually two groups: the routine group and the no routine group.

I think I belong to my own group, which is my baby's natural routine group. Hopefully, our numbers will grow.

Before I had children, I used to watch people who belonged to the no routine group. The children were always crying, they were hungry as they hadn't eaten yet or were overtired. They would be wide awake at midnight and the parents looked like they would drop dead. The parents also looked stressed and resentful of a lack of quiet time or alone time. Everything seemed all over the place, completely ad hoc.

So, when our first daughter was born, I preached routine. Routine, routine, routine. I wanted each morning to start at the same time. She ate every four hours, not before and not later. She had her naps, and was put to bed at 8pm. She was a really unhappy baby. She was hungry and didn't want to wait. I didn't understand that breastfeeding only works on demand and I was starving her. So, I got convinced to start bottle-feeding; she ate but was still miserable. My naptimes didn't work as she wanted different times, and then we put her to bed at our scheduled bedtime and spent AGES trying to get her to sleep so that my husband and I could have some time together. *Stress*! My god, it was stressful. I spent my time in catch up mode and always went to bed feeling like I was failing parenting.

Soon, God entered into it. Life as we knew it threw caution to the wind, we moved, we were on the road, we had no structure as it was impossible. It was the best thing that ever happened.

Now, this doesn't mean we had no routine, we just put some time into structuring our own routine, what worked for us, for our babies and what made us feel good. Most importantly we watched our children for what their needs were at the time, and trust me, their needs are always changing.

When your baby is first born, he will need to eat a lot, and then he will sleep a lot. No eating = no sleeping. But if you're watching, suddenly after that first six weeks, he'll make a shift. He'll suddenly miss a feeding or sleep through it. You'll know because your breasts will be so full you'll want to wake him up to feed. Then he'll start sleeping longer at night. From what at the starting point seemed like a seamless stream of childhood, you will be aware of each week seeming different.

Who They Really Are

Following your baby's cues will make life easy and stress free. Then try to stay one step in front of his game plan. If he usually falls asleep at 1pm, feed him at 12:30 so he has a good sleep. If he falls asleep at night around 8pm, make sure he's eaten well just before. Don't leave it to him being in a total state before feeding or putting him to bed. Then both of you will be upset. Watch his own routine and follow it. He'll probably change it, but that just means when you offer him milk one day he won't be interested. That's okay, keep an eye out for him looking tired, and then feed him.

The only thing to watch for is to make sure you keep focused on your child. This is how to avoid the crying, hungry, fussy baby that will stress you out. Sometimes, that important phone call has to wait five minutes while you feed your baby or put him down to sleep. Sometimes, you have to be a little late getting somewhere. Sometimes, paperwork can be thought on a little bit longer. Watch yourself saying, "I'll just get this done first," and remember, you'll do a much better job when your baby is happy and comfortable. So, take the time out and go with the flow of it all. The only thing that falls outside of that is making sure you eat yourself. Try to eat before you get starving, so if your baby decides to completely change schedules and surprise you, you'll be able to stop yourself from fainting or getting stressed.

So, I guess what I'm saying with the routine issue, is relax with it. It won't do any future damage if your baby doesn't go to bed at a certain time now, or if your baby sleeps better with you rather than in his crib. Follow what feels right to you and listen to your baby and you will have a happy home.

A Happy Home. That is the result of spiritual parenting. And at this point, spiritual parenting is simply listening to your baby as pure, positive energy and keeping yourself in a feeling good place and connected as often as possible.

Health and nutrition

Whether you breastfeed or bottle feed or a bit of both, is entirely up to you. Like I said in the previous section, go with what feels good to you and what brings you the feeling of relief and well being. Before you make any choices regarding nutrition for your infant, including what to feed him, when to introduce solids, how he feels about food etc., check with your feeling about the situation. Follow your instincts and your special connection with your child. You will know when it's the right time to introduce food, and what that food should be. Don't let marketing or other people's advice bog you down, watch yourself in everything you are being told and if it feels *off*, walk in the other direction.

Around four months, the subject of vaccinations will be coming up when talking to your health practitioner. This subject seems to be raising more concerns lately, so I thought I would touch on it briefly regarding how to approach it from a Good Feeling place, and from the place of Source.

Your child's health becomes your number one concern even before he is born. Of course, you want him beaming with vitality and rarely sick. Of course, when you think of the diseases that are out there, it makes you shudder and you would do anything to protect him. Vaccinations are a strong antidote when faced with those fears. On the flip side, it seems there is something unnatural in introducing small quantities of a disease and chemicals in order to trick your baby's little body into building resistance against them. Back and forth the argument goes between doctors, parents, natural health practitioners, and media coverage. No matter what your belief, you will find arguments to back up that belief. So as a parent, what are you to do?

No matter what, you have to go with what feels good. No matter what, you have to go with what you feel certain about. My husband and I felt secure in the strength of our children's natural immunity and didn't have them vaccinated. The idea of it felt very *off* to us. However, it took some soul searching to know we couldn't go through with it. We did the research and then we did the soul search. You might do the research and feel it's what you should do. The truth is that if you don't, you won't feel good about it. You don't want to be watching your child, wondering if you made the wrong choice, wondering if he'll "catch it." You have to go to what you know, what feels best. Follow what feels good to you and trust that it will be well.

Meditation and back to Source

From here on, I will start mentioning meditation, which is probably what anyone picking up a book regarding spiritual parenting has in mind. I'm not going to suggest teaching your baby to meditate. Not only would it cause stress and be impossible, it would be unnecessary as he is still so close to his Source, that it would seem repetitive to him even if he could understand it. However, for the first years of your child's life, I do find it important to make space for some calm, meditative time in your life. Creating an atmosphere of the divine can be a sanctuary for you and your baby. It creates a safe feeling that as they get older they will seek out themselves. At this age, this can simply be done with lighting candles in a dark room for a cranky baby. It can be deep breathing as you put him to sleep. It can even be singing gentle Oms, if this feels comfortable to you, rather than a lullaby. It depends on your situation and lifestyle. With our daughters, we were living a very chaotic life. People were around all the time, and then we were moving, on the road a lot etc. We made a habit of lighting candles and incense and my husband would rock them to sleep in their car seats, slowly swinging it to some music. It was a beautiful, calm experience. However, with our son, the need hasn't been there. If he's cranky, taking him out to our sun porch is enough to ground him. Making him laugh connects him as much as any sacred space time. Therefore, look to ground your child, or moments to help him connect to his Source in times of being chaotic. That is the perfect introduction to spiritual awareness from an early age, simply providing contrasting feeling spaces.

Toys and products

This may sound silly to you, but I want to talk about the spiritual effect of clothes. No, seriously. By spiritual effect I mean something that separates your baby from Source in the forms of frustration, anxiety and irritation, aka. uncomfortable clothing.

Now, I'm not saying not to dress up your baby in his or her Sunday best when you're going out, and I'm not saying that

Who They Really Are

he has to remain in sleepers until he's old enough to express discomfort. Rather, I would like to draw your attention to how your baby's clothes feel to him. It's an important practice when looking at clothing to use your imagination and try to feel what the clothes would feel like. Get inside your baby's skin. Are there any stiff tags at the neck or legs? Are the seams rough or stiff? Also, are there transfers and images that aren't covered over from the inside or are the stitches exposed to the skin? Your baby doesn't care if there's a great Winnie the Pooh image on his pj's, if it means that it is constantly rubbing him when he's on his stomach. Also, material is important. Both my husband and I hate wool as it makes our skin itch, so none of our children have worn it unless it has a lining or they have a few layers on. We are also aware of fleece as it doesn't breathe and can be itchy when you wear it under blankets. Fleece also has the strange ability to cause electric shocks if the air is dry. We really try to keep it to cotton or linens, just for pure comfort sake. However, this doesn't mean dump it all and start with a new wardrobe. Rather, imagine what each piece feels like, and see if wearing a t-shirt underneath would make a difference, or if you can cut tags out or modify in other ways to make comfort a priority for your baby.

Around two-three months you'll naturally start showing your baby various things. Keep in mind that you want the toys to add to his observations and not distract from them. Nowadays, there are so many gadgets and electrical components to toys, I even bought a simple bouncy chair for our son when he was born and had to disconnect a vibration setting. It just seemed unnatural to let a vibrating current run through our son's chair. I am our children's nightmare if they want battery operated things, and this is more prevalent when they are under a year. Maybe under two years. The world is a beautiful place, and I love to watch them explore it. I can't help but feel that the flashing lights and noisy beeps put a distraction in the way of experiencing natural wonder. Therefore, watch yourself when toy shopping. Follow what feels good, and if you like the expression on your child's face.

A film came out in 2009 that contained the line, "I love my baby, why would I want to push him away from me?" spoken by a character when presented with a stroller as a gift. Suddenly, stroller sales dropped and there was a mad rush on slings and snugglies. Scores of people now swear to the bonding experience of wearing your child rather than wheeling him around. One doctor even states it makes them smarter. I pondered the whole sling thing when our last child was born, and even though lots of family members loved them, I opted for the stroller. Although I did occasionally grab a snugglie in those early days, when I needed to do something with my arms, it rarely got used after two months had passed. I couldn't get over how insecure I felt. Basically, I felt that my use of the sling would be overshadowed by my fear of the possibilities of either our son falling out of one side, or suffocating on the other side. Also, I felt that my relaxed state present with the possibilities of grabbing the car seat and plopping it into a stroller when I was out, without our baby even waking up, was too important. But then... I started baby wearing our son at a late 22 months, as we were traveling and I felt he would feel insecure low down in a stroller around a lot of strangers. He loved it, and soon learnt the word "Ergo" to ask to go in it. Now, I wish I had had it from the beginning. I've passed my Ergo on to two nephews since and their mom's have sworn by it. In this, and all things manufactured for bonding benefits, I have to say, follow your instincts and what makes you feel the most relief, but try a carrier before leaving them for good. Research the newer ones, and allow yourself to explore lots of options. The feeling that you are emitting, either the joy or relief of the stress and tension is what affects your baby, not whether he is in a chair with wheels or strung on your back. I have had great fun talking and babbling with a baby in his stroller with his car seat making it face me. I've also heard calls of joy from a baby looking around him and exploring on his own from his stroller. I've also had incredible relief breastfeeding on the go! So, what I'm saying is, your joy is your baby's joy; your stress, your baby's stress. Your baby knows the language of emotions and intention. He will only feel pushed away in a stroller if that's what you feel about it. He has no framework to come up with an intention like that out of nowhere. He gets his framework of how he feels from how you feel. Your baby will feel secure knowing you are there, knowing you love him and seeing your joy-filled, stress-free face. That is the bonding experience. Do whatever it takes to make sure that's what he sees daily.

There is also the question of playpen or freedom. I've never felt like a playpen was a jail but I know a lot of people do. I simply see it as a room within a room, like letting them explore a little bit at a time. As your baby gets older, he will need space to play and make observations, and it's nice to be able to set him up with that rather than follow him around everywhere, stopping him from getting into all your stuff. The stress of wondering if he's safe becomes his stress but when you know he's happy and you relax, he relaxes into being happy. Stay connected to how you feel, thereby creating your own parenting experience.

You, as Parent, You as YOU

And yes, this is YOUR experience. Oh, I'm not saying your baby isn't experiencing with you, but he's experiencing his own flipside of the coin right now. Also, he is entirely in the moment. Ah, that might be worth repeating. YOUR BABY IS ENTIRELY IN THE MOMENT.

He has no sense of time. He has no idea of the future and no thought to yesterday. Unless you have a definite day to day routine, like breakfast at the same time, or how you change him, or the fact that he sits in his bouncy chair every evening, every day is a new adventure, a new experience to him. There is no waiting concept, that's why he freaks out so much with every sign of hunger, or even tiredness; if it's not alleviated right away, this is like his new forever. However, his joy is felt in fullness, without conditions. Oh, isn't that how life is supposed to be? Isn't that how it should be for all of us?

Now, with this comes a very hard pill for us parents to swallow. This time, this wonderful, beautiful time, he won't remember. There is no way about it. Now, this can be really helpful for those bad days. I shudder to think of some of my bad days during my first baby experiences, but they don't know those days happened. In fact, however poignant I thought some events were to them prior to them being three, it always startles me when I find out our daughters have no clue what I am talking about.

So, don't worry. Be the parent you want to be. Try it on for size and feel good. Some people might read, "Oh, she's saying hit my kid, and he won't remember it." No, he won't remember it, but would that be what makes you feel good? Of course not. Feeling good is connected to Source. Source is pure positive energy, and how could any action out of anger or frustration feel good? Rather, I'm saying set yourself free. If you had a bad day and didn't act as you wanted, if you left your baby crying for a bit longer, or couldn't stand it and threw a pot of rice at the wall, then go to bed tonight and think of the wonderful things you appreciate, think of feeling good, and know tomorrow will be better.

Now, saying a baby doesn't remember what happens in babyhood doesn't mean it doesn't matter to the baby either. This is the foundation building of his childhood. When else would it start if not now? This is the creation of the default system he'll rely on. You can't postpone this until he's about three and then decide it's time for a happy house. Well, you can, but it won't seem as stable to him as it would from now. Therefore, if he is a baby in a house of screaming and anger, then that is what he'll expect, that is what he'll vibrate with, that is what will be his response. If he is a baby in a house full of comfort, full of love, full of laughter, THAT will be his default, and for the rest of his life that will be what he expects, that will be his foundation, his starting point. What a difference.

There is also the question of the Law of Attraction. It's a funny thing when looking at your life which suddenly has another attraction point. I don't know when a baby really starts attracting his own reality, but I would say it's very early on. I know that I can be having a good, grounded, happy day, but our son could have had a tummy ache the night before and the rest of the day seems to go wrong for him. From banging his head, bumping a hand and having more meltdowns than seems possible for a usual happy-go-lucky guy, it's obvious that he's not attracting a good outcome. The only way to fix it is to make him giggle, make him laugh, tickle his toes and then put him down for a nap. Hopefully, he'll wake up feeling more himself, having gone to sleep in a jiving, connected, happy place.

This is where parenting takes an interesting angle. You have your spiritual experience in this physical body and your baby has his. However, you are intermingled. You affect his perspective, his experience. Also, his can affect yours too. This is the time to experiment with yourself. Hold yourself in a grounded position as much as possible and set him on his feet running. This can be as simple as making him smile, and breaking the spiral of feeling cranky.

Dealing with tiredness and how to live without sleep

Sleep can sometimes feel like a stranger to you. Around the third or fourth month your baby will have gotten over any colic, but teething is starting to hit. You comfort and comfort and comfort, love, love, love, but sometimes you could just walk into something for feeling tired.

Time for re-perspective. I know, at this rate of tiredness you might scream if I say, "Find a good feeling thought," one more time. So, I won't. I'll just think it.

Let's look at sleep and the forgotten world of needing eight hours to function. I really felt relief when I heard Abraham Hicks' description of what sleep is (Abraham is a group of spiritual teachers channeled thru the brilliant Esther Hicks, definitely worth a look at): Sleep is when you and the greater part of you become one. When you let go of any resistance, any contrast, and join your non-physical self again. It is a time of connection. How you feel after that, or even how you dream through it, are indicators to how connected you feel in your day to day life. Now, the clincher of this is that you don't need as much sleep as you think. They suggest a four-hour sleep time maximum, but I do love bed so much I find that hard. However, I also find it hard to reprogram my brain to accept that it's natural to have little sleeps more than once a day. It's kind of like check in points for your soul. You don't need the sleep for your body as much as for your spirit. Now saying that, I know you feel tired, but play with me for a moment.

I've put this to the test, especially since right now I write at night and am up until the wee hours of the morning. There are days when I repeat constantly, "I'm so tired, I really need a nap. I'm so tired." The more I say it the tired-er I feel. However, then I might get an idea to write about, or something might make me jive and I get a burst of energy. Often at one in the morning I'm dancing about. What an ideal thing for a new mother. If you feel tired, follow your baby's schedule and sleep when he sleeps, if he won't sleep, simply pull out of the woodwork a good feeling thought, make them bubble, something with energy. Don't contradict them, simply put your imagination to work and feel better.

Appreciation, good feeling thoughts, watching how you feel at all times, interaction with your baby, eye contact and love, love, love. This is the only exercise needed for this time in babyhood.

I know I've gone into some pragmatics, which might throw people off a bit. However, the way I see it, there are great spiritual benefits to everyone if you find ways to limit stress. You can't be stressed and stay connected. So, eliminate the stress as much as possible and have fun with this time. These six months pass so quickly, enjoy, and feel good with that little bundle in your arms.

A guide to being a spiritually aware parent

Affirmation

The world is a beautiful place and I am forever reminded of its wonder when looking at it through your new eyes. Thank you for choosing me, dear one. Thank you for letting me be part of your experience. Let us look at life together. As your senses awaken to each new blissful wonder, I stand as the observer to your new awareness. You fill the world with newness for me. And, it is indeed a better place, the perfect place, now that you are in it. Sometimes, I need to just take a breather, just to fully appreciate the wonder you have brought me.

Chapter 7

Six months to one year

The Little Explorer

What's happening in your baby's world

Oh, isn't the world a wonderful place? There are things to pick up, food to eat, people to laugh with, animals to watch, and the ever-growing exploration of this body and how it moves. Even a shadow dancing on a wall fills your little explorer with sweet satisfaction.

For him, there is no danger, no conflict and basically no Nos. It is the age of wonder. However, for you, it is the beginning of the age of contrast and the time of terror. How do you find the balance to let him experience all the wonder and magic of the world before him, yet keep him alive to see his first birthday? You simply can't, by any logic or instinct, let him eat every crumb on the floor, tear up every piece of paper or pull all the hair out of the dog. Suddenly, you are thrown into the land of No, and neither you nor your baby likes it. This means suddenly that your baby will experience more contrast to what he wants, and his desire will become stronger. I don't think the desire to eat dirt will become stronger because he has experienced the contrast of not being allowed to; however, his desire to explore will become stronger and that is a good thing.

Therefore, this time needs to be focused on two things, the Contrast and The Art of Distraction.

Behaviour

As we talked about in the introduction of this book, we, as Pure, Positive, Beings, experience contrast in order to know what we really want. Contrast creates desire in which we can expand. This is the time of your baby's contrast, as he often picks up things or tries to go places he really can't. As you prevent him from getting what he asks for or wants, you become his contrast, and he cries. Oh boy, does he wail and this is what gives birth to that phrase the terrible twos, when NO is the operative word.

There is nothing easier than to fall into a "no, no, no, no, no," drum habit, and this age is a good time to train yourself to not fall into it. It's not such a problem now, but as the years go by, you will find yourself saying no automatically and wondering later what harm would have been done by simply saying yes sometimes. Therefore, be the contrast with your No, but be the quick connection with an alternative Yes. Babies love yeses. They love to see you smile, they love to receive praise, they love to achieve goals like standing at the side of their crib or getting to the other side of a room, and they love acknowledgment of how they are progressing. So, rather than putting the focus on, "Oh my god, he's now a little terror into everything," it is time to make mountains out of the little things we take for granted. It's time to notice the magic around us, and it's time to play. This will keep your baby's focus on being happy and not getting frustrated. It will also provide him with the security that although you are sometimes contrasting what he wants, you are providing a world that is fun and wonderful to be part of.

Remember that in your baby's world, simplicity is key. He's literally connected to Source or Not connected to Source, and he will switch quickly between the two. The states are easy to recognize, happy baby is connected, upset baby is unconnected, or experiencing contrast.

Therefore, always have a Yes for every No, and avoid using the word No at least part of the time. Expand his vocabulary and understanding early and when he approaches something dangerous or even just not baby safe, then say it belongs to someone else, such as "Daddy's" or "Mommy's" then quickly pass him something that is his. Have a supply of board books, small toys and stuffed animals around that you can whip out wherever you are, and say his name when you pass it to him. The concept of ownership may take some time for him to understand, but it will make the No stage so much easier. Also, keep a supply of things out of general view, so when you pull them out, your baby will be really interested in them rather than have the attitude of "Come on, I've seen this so often. I want something more interesting!" Yes, it's okay to give things that aren't toys, for a period of time our son loves empty wipe boxes, but beware that every time you give something like that, he will think that everyone like it is his.

Remember, your baby uses the language of emotion rather than words. Therefore, as an introduction to vocabulary, use the language of how something feels. If he's putting something in his mouth that's disgusting, cringe up your face, stick out your tongue and say "blah." Be consistent and say it if something makes it to his mouth and he knows it tastes awful. Then give him something better to chew on, or a snack and he will know his desire is being met well.

This is the basic introduction to the Art of Distraction, which becomes more elaborate as you look for more things to distract all of your baby's senses and stop the drive to just wreak havoc.

You can also distract your baby by pointing out things to look at rather than grab. Pets are fascinating, as long as you can trust them to not attack your baby if his interest in them gets too close at some point when you aren't watching. Looking at anything in the outside world can momentarily distract a child so you can get him out of harm's way. Birds, trees, flowers, your baby is still very sensitive to the energy emitting from any life form. Family members can provide great distraction as they might make a funny face or say hi while you move your baby away from the No activity he was about to take part in. Even water dripping from a tap, your baby's and your shadow dancing on the wall, his reflection in the mirror, fire in a fire place, snow, rain, sun, wind, or the reflection of the light on a soup spoon. All of it fascinates your baby's mind and imagination. Also, all of this helps your child become curious about his world in a more focused, proactive way.

Who They Really Are

No matter what, your baby is going to be interested in whatever you are doing. Therefore, simple things like using your computer, talking on the phone, or getting something from the fridge can prove to be frustrating for you as your baby leans over to grab at whatever you've got. This is an ongoing problem; however, it can be alright with a bit of a mental shift from you and a bit of distraction. It makes perfect sense that something like a computer, with its flashing lights and quick images, is going to be something your baby is anxious to explore. Same with phones with the voice of whomever you're talking to coming mysteriously from the other end. In fact, from a baby's perspective these everyday things are magic. Try to refocus on that perspective and understand why it causes so much fascination. Then, I would suggest distract, distract, distract!

Your intention is everything and what your focus is defines the energy you are emitting. In turn, that energy is what your baby reads from you. Therefore, when your darling is stressing you out with his explorations, try to spend some moments in his perspective before seeing him as a problem. We can easily fall into the trap of perceiving our children as common denominators. "Oh, he's a baby." "That's the age". "Terrible twos start young." When really, when we see our children as the spirits, the people they really are, we can remember what their intention is. When our intention is to understand them, we can still guide them away from danger or even things that we don't want them into, and they will read our intention as what's best for them. When we just sigh and pull them away, we become the contrast they resist against and that sets up a system of resistance which can last a very long time.

I often suggest to parents that they spend some time within their child's perception. When they are asleep, or are feeding in your arms, simply close your eyes and imagine seeing the world through their eyes. Ask yourself, Your True self, to tap into their truest essence, and just feel it for a bit. You will find it easier to understand and deal with your child's explorations, when you can see the world through their new eyes.

One last thing, there seems to be a crying cycle with babies that's important to get to know. When a crying fit happens, for sometime after that he will remain sensitive to what has upset him. If you put him down at that point, chances are he'll begin to wail as soon as his feet touch the floor. So, hug him that little bit longer, dance with him, play with him, and distract him from what he's not getting. Then refocus him on something new when you put him down. Also, don't get into the habit of only picking up your child when he cries. If he seems to be losing focus on what he's doing, or gives you that look of "What are you doing? I'm getting kind of bored." Pick him up for a cuddle. This will stop any idea that he has to cry in order to get your attention, and in the long run will deplete any whining habits.

If only dealing with contrast was this easy for all of us. If only by using the simple art of distraction we could simply refocus back to our spiritual centre. But then again, maybe it is that easy.

Routine

Action, action, moving, moving. With so much energy to explore being used, why is it that sometimes they are so hard to get to sleep? Within the first six months your baby will have slept quite a lot of the time away. However, as he heads into the second half of his first year, suddenly that won't come as easily. There can be a number of reasons, from being too full he doesn't want milk and that's how he usually falls asleep, to the stimulation of the world around him and him wanting to explore it.

The art of putting a child to sleep is sometimes a difficult one. However, it is a spiritual one. Remember, sleep is when we and our spirits join without resistance. Your baby is suddenly so in his body. He loves it. He's playing, he's laughing, he's exploring. Sometimes he looks as if he's saying, who needs sleep? However, it's important for him and for you that he gets some shut eye, so ease him into it gently.

There were times with our first two that I got so anxious if they wouldn't go to sleep. I swear, I would rock them so fast sometimes that there was never a chance they would fall asleep. I guess I was trying to wear them out, but all I did was get tired myself. So, I soon learned that it is about breath and about stillness.

Remember your breathing exercises from pregnancy? Breathing fully and letting your tummy rise with each inhalation will naturally lull your baby to sleep. Doing this slowly is actually the state of breathing as when we sleep, so tuning into that will change your baby's breathing pattern and make him relaxed and sleepy. Any lullaby you pick, sing it using this same pace and breathing technique.

No matter what, getting stressed about sleep is the way to have a baby awake forever. He has to know you are secure and alright before he crashes for the night. So, before you head for bedtime, make him laugh, look at a book, tell him he's wonderful.

It is said that if you go to sleep in a state of appreciation or a state of feeling good, you will wake up in the same state. Well, what goes for you also goes for you small child, so put him to bed feeling secure, happy and in a state of appreciation for the life he has chosen with you.

You'll probably notice that suddenly your 7-9 month old isn't content to just stay in your arms or even quiet down to go to sleep. It doesn't matter how tired you think he is, he'll push away from you and try to get off to go explore again. How frustrating! You have naptime set aside to get a few things done but he just isn't co-operating. How do you stay grounded in a good feeling place? First, breathe. He'll go to sleep soon enough and maybe he'll even crash for longer than usual because he's worn himself out. Put him somewhere safe, like a playpen, and go about some picking up or things easy to stop again when he's ready. Follow his lead and let him explore, just be aware of his overtired state and make sure he's extra safe from anything about; he'll probably fall easily. The minute he gets cranky, try him for some sleep again. Keep focused more on your state of being, than his. Don't do anything that if he tries to grab at something, or explore something, you'll get frustrated, such as being on the computer or writing down something. Things can always wait until he does feel it's time to sleep. Relax into it. This may be sign of a new routine coming, or just a one-off experience due to teething or fussiness. Don't give in to the panic of it getting in your way. This is just one of the challenges that are on the parenting road, let it ride, be easy with it and breathe.

You might be being told by family or friends that at this point if your child is having problems going to sleep to "let them cry it out." I have serious problems with this. I must admit I tried this technique when I was first a parent and surrendered to my stress. I worried about spoiling our child, and habits I wouldn't be able to break. Now, I realize nothing made me feel worse. I would be near tears as our baby cried in the next room and then I would spend the night guilt ridden if indeed she did fall asleep without knowing I was always there for her. I would literally want to wake her up to hug her, to tell her it was alright, and that I loved her. "Crying it out" is like telling your child to toughen up, forget about whatever he is feeling and do as you want no matter what. It always feels so *off*. If your child cries a lot in bed, there are a number of possible reasons why. One, he doesn't know how close you are to him and feels insecure there, so let him sit and play in bed while you are cleaning up around it in the day time. Let him have a bit of fun there. In the day, don't wait until he cries to pick him up so that he knows it doesn't take a big scene to get your attention. Make sure he has some action before bedtime, let him crawl for a bit and get some wearing out time, then calm him down, feed him to the point of stuffing, and then have some quality time. Read him a book, sing some songs, look at some beautiful things, make him laugh a little bit, or smile. Then, let him gently go to sleep, with the knowledge that he lives in a beautiful and peaceful place, with people that love him. It will be there when he wakes up, so he might as well sleep and restore himself. Also, remember to use your own emotional guidance system. If ever it feels right to let him cry it out, then by all means do it, but I have a funny feeling there's a small chance that would ever happen.

I would also like to add that co-sleeping can decrease a lot of stress at bedtime. Rather than a battle over getting a child to stay in their own bed, sleep becomes a free, lucid thing. I had problems releasing the concept of sleep and bedtime for awhile, until I read something that asked why would our children know about the concept of time? Of course they wouldn't, and the only reason to understand that concept is to keep to a world's schedule. When a baby co-sleeps and feels us asleep, the flow of rest comes naturally. Now, I always had our babies in cribs when we weren't in bed, for my sense of security, but a family bed on the floor has worked for many people. Once again, find your feel good space on this topic as with any other.

<u>Health and nutrition</u>

What you feed your baby and how you feed have a direct connection to how he feels, how he stays connected and how he stays feeling good.

Of course, it is logical to say fresh and natural is best. When our daughters were little, they had the best organic vegetables money could buy, they had limited sweets, were (and still are) vegetarian and were the pictures of health. Our son has had this too, but we've found another element that makes him burble. He LOVES food. He is fascinated by everything about it. He will happily watch it being prepared and he will easily try anything. However, we've also noticed he wants what we eat. Trying to feed him a jar of baby food with a spoon was like pulling teeth. It can be the best on the market, but it still has little flavour and it still means he's not eating with the family. Yet, from seven months on, stick a plate of mashed potatoes and a few mashed carrots in front of him and he will stuff himself as he watches us all eat the same thing. He laughs as he looks across at his sisters and knows that he is acting grown up. This craving to be part of the family at mealtimes started from four months on; however, we did allow nature to give some cues and didn't give him anything until teething set in and a tooth had started to emerge. When he did start, he beamed, and it has made mealtime as a family affair even more important.

No matter what, at any age a hungry child will moan more and be cranky. It needs to be the first on your checklist for a long number of years. Snacks will keep everyone cheerful. For a baby this age, resort to bananas, bread, or the great baby rice cakes that are now on the market. Also, if you bake, a plain muffin or cake provides a great filler as well as good entertainment.

There is so much talk about allergies and sensitivities now, sometimes you wonder if you should feed your child anything. Look at your food and decide whether it's in as natural a state as you can get it. Refinement is a big culprit for reactions, be it refined white flour or refined sugar. Both of these can be resolved if you can find a white flour that is stone-ground or switching to whole wheat and there are unrefined sugars that are easy to find on the market. The reason that refinement is so potent is due to the fact that things are removed from the food and then some artificially reintroduced to them. This makes it hard for the body to recognize and can cause a reaction.

Stick to as natural as you can and adopt the attitude that food is your friend, there to be enjoyed by both you and your baby. Introducing a friendly and happy approach to food to your child will reap a lifetime of happy eating and healthy living.

People start to look at weaning a baby anywhere between six months to two years, although some mothers have felt best breastfeeding for later than that, even up to the age of five or six. Of course, then there are those like me, ending up on the surprise journey of child led weaning. In this subject, like most you will have noticed, I feel you have to follow your own truth. There is no right or wrong, simply you, feeling around to find the best feel good option. Weaning can give a lot of stress to both you and your baby or it can be a natural occurrence that gradually takes place between you and your child. It all depends on the approach you take, whether it comes from fear and distrust or from love and trust. It sometimes seems that your brain gets riddled with "shoulds" and "shouldn'ts," or if you're like me "should I? or "shouldn't I?" With our daughters, I approached breastfeeding, and bottles, from a place of lack. In other words, I kept doubting when they should be having it, when they shouldn't be, whether I was getting into a deep hole, whether habits were being formed that would be hard to break. I had my feet firmly planted in a place of the future and of worry. Needless to say, I didn't attract easy weanings or transitions. However, with our son, I learnt to let go and it's amazing to watch nature at work. Yes, sometimes I felt like it was never going to end, but it was a chaotic time, of unsettled living, a time of running a business and my busy mind. Nursing him until he was five wasn't something I set out to do, but something that provided him a space of security, a mom time, which kept him grounded in chaos. One day he just knew, it was over. He moved into his own room and planned to stop. He managed to go to sleep without it, and then after a few nights, I was dried up and the choice was gone. He never looked back. I wish I'd been as trusting as he was.

Trust in nature and your child with the weaning process; avoid using breastfeeding as a substitute for spending creative time with your child or just as a way to shut him up so you can focus on something else. Also, please, please avoid just sitting on your phone during a cuddle time. It's not always about the milk, it's about You and Him.. You can trust that one day down the line, your child will decide that he no longer needs nature and your baby knows exactly what is best, all you have to do is trust and follow the signs of change.

Now saying that, your feel good place is just as important as your baby's, so if suddenly it feels incredibly *off* to breastfeed, breathe, relax and start the weaning process that works for you. Something suddenly turning *off* indicates that the time has past and shifted, so trust your connection to everything you are, and shift towards the new experience.

Sickness, colds and flus

There's nothing more upsetting than seeing your child get his first cold or flu. Aside from hating to see them suffer and be miserable, your whole routine and way of life gets thrown off and really you wonder if it will ever be normal again. However, saying that, there is also something so incredibly bonding about your child getting sick. Perhaps the need of this bonding time created the sickness in the first place. Therefore, don't fight against it; take advantage of it. Even if he's heavy, carry him everywhere, let him sleep in your arms, let him stay up until he zonks out, drop everything and make him feel better by making him smile and laugh. It is amazing how a sick child won't wallow in his sickness at this age and for a brief moment will crack a smile or give way to a belly laugh with a funny look from you. Suddenly, all the exploring is given up to having special time with you, to feel safe again, even though his body is going through weird things. It's like the security of his body and surroundings suddenly become unreliable, so make sure you are the safety net. For some reason whenever a child is sick, after he is well, he will always look a little bit older, proving that growth and expansion has occurred. So, steal these precious moments, turn off the phone, let him feel that everything is okay. It sets him back on his feet running, and quite frankly it fills you up with sweet satisfaction and makes you feel great, rather than the frustration experienced by someone who is trying to run the show like normal in spite of having a sick child, ("And damn it, why won't he sleep in his bed", or "For heaven sake, can't I put him down for one minute.") See what I mean? He'll be over it, and grown out of being carried and cared for soon enough.

As a parent, sickness can always bring out a fear factor in you as well. With every bout of diarrhea or vomiting, stories of dehydration, hospitalization or even death will start to resurface in your mind. Treat this as you did in pregnancy and know that that was in common denominator studies (not even that common) and you don't live under those rules. Treat your child's body responsibly, with plenty of water and healthy foods. If you are still breastfeeding, then treat through your breast milk by drinking loads of water yourself and eating well, and then treat yourself well with feeling better thoughts. Your baby needs to get sick every once in awhile in order to build up a stronger immune system. It will pass soon and he will be better for it. His body is healthy and knows what it needs to do. Everything is perfect and will be back to normal soon.

As your baby gets older, you will find that he gets sick more often if he is in a state of disconnection from Who He Really Is. Take this time to find his and your spiritual centre. Make him laugh, take the time to read and play with him until you see his eyes light up with serenity and spiritual groundedness. Not only will he get well faster, but as you start to become aware of signs of disconnection before he gets sick, you will be helping him remain well in both body and spirit on a more regular basis.

Meditation and back to Source

Begin to show the difference between the feeling place of calm and the feeling place of action in your baby. In this time of exploration it is easy to let your baby set the pace of the day to be go, go, go, go, go, go, crash out. Therefore, find points in your day that you can pick your child up, and show him things to capture his attention. If it's a book, let it be of a calm nature, with pretty pictures rather than bold. Don't bother reading the words, just point things out in the pictures that your baby might recognize. If not a book, then point out things around him, play with soft, quiet toys and let your baby's focus go from the broad scale to the minuscule.

Imagine your daily life as a piece of well-crafted music. Nothing is more aggravating than an album that sets one pace, plays one rhythm and goes on, and on, and on. A good album will take you on a journey through different paces and feelings, sometimes fast and fun, and then dropping into a song of calm and delicate peace. Listen to your house and see it in this light and offer this to you and your baby. Times of calm always work well when your baby is getting tired, or after an hour of action. After an hour, even shifting to calm for 10 minutes or so will set him back to exploration mode with new focus.

Fun and games

This is the time of fun and play, and as a parent this can really unleash your inner child. However, what games are suitable for this young age of exploration.

Often we over complicate matters as parents. We look for the things that would entertain us and make it all too big of a deal for our little explorers, who find the smallest thing wonderfull. Start by taking cues from traditions and play some peek-a-boo, which is a great trust building game. One second you are gone, the next you are back, instilling a sense of patience in your baby if you happen to be out of the room for a minute. Also pat-a-cake is a good action game to introduce. What's great about this one is that your child has to sit still to partake. It shows that no matter how much he can and wants to move, entertainment can be done in different ways. Ride a cock horse became a standard in our house at this time and the girls were asking for it from their father up until a couple of years ago. Action nursery rhymes are a great introduction to a number of things and will inspire lots of moments of pure, belly laughter.

When you are trying to get some quiet sit-down time with your child, show him simple activities. Get a pail or small box and put some of his teething toys in it, then shake it about and dump them out. Put them back in, then dump them out. Your baby will soon try to copy it. Bang on the bottom of the pail or box like a drum, and let your baby try. Stack up blocks, (cloth ones, plastic or if your child is over 10 months wooden ones with soft edges) and then show him how to knock them down, then stack them up again.

Take a stuffed toy and show your baby how to pretend to feed it with feeding noises (such as num, num, num etc.) also, get the toy to do some of the action poems once your baby knows they exist.

Play with shadows on the wall, look at your fingers and toes, speak through a paper tube, pat your mouth while saying Ah and make it vibrate. Find a soft ball or plastic cup and roll it about between you and your baby.

Basically, look at the world through your baby's eyes and see the possibility of play, and introduce some imagination to it. Have fun and remember, every game you show your baby he'll remember and be more likely to try it himself. Repeat it a few times and soon you will find him sitting there, playing exactly what you introduced to him, or trying to anyway. Watch for the signs of him trying to mimic a game or activity and then jump on board with him. This could come in terms of clapping or doing the Way Up action in pat-a-cake, or trying to "high 5," he might try hitting a drum, or rolling a ball. If you take his cues and follow his game plan, then you are telling him you understand and you will listen to him. It stops it from becoming about always doing what you tell him to do and re-enforces the co-creating partnership you established when pregnant. Your baby will feel that he is doing well, learning and expanding, and that you are ready to help him grow, and appreciating everything he has to offer. It will also make any no more concrete for him as he will know you usually say yes, so no's are for a reason.

Toys and products

For the busiest little explorer, a playpen just won't pen him in. By eight months he wants to crawl about and explore and really stretch his muscles and the playpens of today seem to make this impossible. Standing up is difficult as they dip at the sides and the mesh is hard to see through when the light shines a certain way. However, it is rather stressful to have a baby wandering everywhere unless your house is baby proofed to the point of having nothing of any danger or value stored lower than three feet. We came up with a solution that works amazingly, but would need to be modified by anyone who has a house where looking pretty is a high priority. We made an 8x4 pen, about two feet high out of 2x4s and then put plastic sheeting between the posts on the sides, we then stuck the great interlocking foam tiles you get from Walmart and other stores on the floor. Our son loved it from nine months old, which was a bit of a surprise as he was just getting use to wandering around a bit. We had an odd assortment of toys in there, and we rearranged it and changed it as he's grown and his needs changed. Our older girls still often jump in with him, or I do. He can wander around the sides to see what everyone is doing. It keeps him part of the house but completely out of danger. I think this could be modified to suit a smaller room, even by making it collapsible, with hinges etc. However, no matter how much of an eyesore it might be, it's nice to know he's safe and happy for the next few months while he gets his feet under him and learns how to live a little safer.

This is the time when toys really do become introduced, but your child doesn't need all the latest things. In fact, some parents find even some household things can provide enough entertainment. I, on the other hand, love toys and have too much fun looking at them and trying them out to really knock them off the list. However, you don't need all the flashy things or take the shopping spree too seriously. As a parent who is looking for spiritually conscious children, I try to find toys with calming colours, soft fabrics, and pretty images. So often baby things are in bold, bright colors, created under the philosophy that they are easier for a baby to see clearly. But I feel that sight and the other senses are ways of interpreting energy and that I would sooner introduce calm, pretty and delicate energies to our children first rather than clear and in-your-face ones.

From the age of six months here's what I suggest:

- An activity board (something with things that spin, flip, or can be turned. Fisher Price made a great one in the 80s and honestly for every child I've had I've been able to hunt one out. It's not got any of the flashy gizmos of current toys, no electronic music or noises, and needs no batteries. It is just a simple board to try things out on.)

- Teething rings etc., which you probably got a few months ago

- Cloth blocks

- Cloth books

- A bath book, which can be used outside the bath

- Some musical instrument, like a baby drum or xylophone, something good to bang on

- A stuffed toy of some sort. They can be fed, put to sleep and made to play pat-a-cake.

- An exersaucer. These are great as your baby has to sit and entertain himself rather than move around.

- Something with wheels that can be pushed and then followed

- Baby plastic beads, to chew and pull apart

- Baby telephone

- By 10 months some Duplo or Mega Blocks, which can be put in a tub and dumped out. Don't put too many in there, as they won't be all played with, just 5-10 pieces.

It's great to be able to tell your baby these things are all his. It will start better respect for your things and give you options for the Art of Distraction. Also, put them in various places, so your baby will be excited to see them each time, rather than having them all in one spot and them getting old.

Cardboard boxes, wipe boxes, cloths, socks, and many other things can also make great toys. As I mentioned before though, just make sure that it's nothing you would mind him touching another one of, so it keeps your baby's world simple.

When your baby starts to really move either by crawling or walking, chances are he's going to fall more than once and chances are he's going to get hurt. There is nothing worse than seeing your child crying in pain over his first fall, his first bump, bruise or cut. However, it has always been interesting for me to watch my reaction. With our first daughter I would often fly off the handle in panic, which would scare her more than the initial fall. I swear, sometimes she almost felt bad for upsetting me so much, even if she was the one to have gotten hurt. How very backward. Now, I know that staying calm and grounded makes getting your child back to Himself again an easy transition. Therefore, pick up your child (unless the fall was so bad that it would be best not to) as quickly as possible, and hug him, hug, hug, hug and give all the comfort you can. Avoid speaking except for telling him it's alright and take him out of the room or area where the accident happened. Once he's calm and looking around in his new surroundings, take the opportunity to see how he is and how hurt he got. If he hasn't stopped crying by this time, you know he's hurt pretty badly, but most of the time you will find this is enough to settle him back to connection. Also, remaining calm and not flying off the handle will keep you connected to Source and exactly where your child needs you.

Holidays and birthdays

There is nothing more exciting for a parent than your baby's first Christmas, Easter or even better, your baby's first birthday. We get all the gear, we throw a party and quite frankly, the baby thinks we've gone completely stark raving mad! There is nothing more rocking to a child's security than a holiday. Other people are around, suddenly you're under stress dealing with company, meals and rushing for gifts, the focus shifts and baby is wondering why all the clamber. Take extra calm and grounding time with your poor little one who is entirely overwhelmed and worried about you. Hold him lots, let him state his needs and breathe. It doesn't matter in the long run if Christmas cards are late, or that one last present needs to be an IOU, your baby feeling good is your number one priority. You know by now that an unhappy baby makes an unhappy you, and then an even unhappier baby. So, give it a few years to expect the bells and whistles to blow. It's worth the price of feeling good.

That's not to say you shouldn't recognize your baby's first year milestone, just be selfish enough to know it's your milestone too. Have a cake, give a present, keep it low key and blissful. Make it a happy day for you, your partner and your child as you celebrate the fact that one year from that date you all came together in this physical time space reality. Do things that bring all of you great pleasure, so that your baby senses it and rejoices in his family's joy over something (even though he'll have no idea what). Avoid the temptation of having a stressful bash, where you will be preparing for hours, and have to entertain loads of people, taking your focus away from the birthday-child. If you feel a party is expected by anyone (and quite frankly you shouldn't feel that, but sometimes we do) then have it another day, after your baby's birthday. This anniversary is the landmark. He's been with you a year. You've been a parent for a year. You've had good days, bad days and just days, but you've grabbed hold of the reins, you've aimed to feel good, and you've jumped onboard for the trip of a lifetime. Take a moment and pat yourself on the back.

You are doing exceptionally well.

You as parent, you as YOU

This time in your baby's life can be a bit frustrating. He explores so fast and wants out of your arms. It is tempting to try to restrict him, but it just takes the life out of his eyes and you feel *off* doing it. However, you continually feel like you have to be refusing him stuff or moving him from danger's way. The Art of Distraction will help you find the feeling good place for yourself as well as him. In fact, playing with your baby can be incredibly therapeutic for both you and your baby on more than one level. I have seen our children being cranky, teething, frustrated and then tired because of it, only to snap back to a joyous life after a few focused moments with me or their father in fun play. It is an amazing feeling to see someone so disconnected and then after helping them focus on fun, immediately become connected. It connects you instantaneously as well. So, now is the time to rediscover your own wonderment, which you will as you look for new and interesting things to grab his attention. PLAY. You might not have played for years, but rediscover the magic of play. It has no goal, no end, no mistakes. So, play, play, play. Enjoy the peals of laughter as you roll with your baby on your bed, get down on the floor and stack things up so he can knock them down, throw things into a pail and take joy in the rattling noise it makes, make funny faces, play with shadows, make a stuffed toy talk or play pat-a-cake. Be the distraction, be the inspiration, so that whatever your child sees or has around him can be his own entertainment. So often, I've seen children surrounded by toys, but never taught how to actually play with them. However, take a bit of time to show them and you might actually be able to steal one or two moments for yourself again.

Ah, yes, time for YOU. This is probably one of the joys of a playpen; a happy explorer can be set up with something and spend half an hour trying to figure out how to use it. In that half an hour, you could have read a book, sat on the front step, talked to a friend and still be able to have a nap when your baby goes for one, or get your chores done then. Take the time to set your baby up, and then reap the benefits yourself.

It has become common parenting advice to tell you to that if you get frustrated or even angry with your baby to put him somewhere and walk out the room for a few minutes, leaving his screams behind you. This has become the usual advice. The problem is that it is simply impossible to find a good feeling place with screams echoing behind you. Chances are, if you are focusing on your baby as Spirit and trying to understand his new vantage point as explorer, you won't get to this point, but if you do, then try to breathe, muster up a smile and the patience, and set him up with something to grab his attention. Then sit for a moment to adjust yourself on a spirit level yourself. Breathe and calm your mind. Then go on an appreciation rampage and I mean appreciate everything, from your shoes to your roof, to the sky over that. Then appreciate that soul who chose you all that time ago to be their mother. Appreciate the fact that at nine months of age, he has been in your arms and physical life the same amount of time that he was within your womb. That may seem a distance away, or like yesterday, but still, life progresses and it will still keep progressing.

As it becomes more expected from your baby that you need your own quiet time and that he will have time alone in a confined space, you will have time to put your focus on other things. Don't ever feel badly about getting time in for yourself. The way I figure it is that it continues the circle that a happy, positive parent makes happy babies, which makes happy parents, which makes… you understand. The attitude of sacrifice and parenting should never be put together. My family has always preached that the best thing about having kids was that they distracted you from yourself, and I've always thought this perspective was a really sad step away from your own journey. What a vantage point to explore new thoughts and new ideas, what a time to look at what you want and who you are, not just under the label "Parent" but as everything you do in this life.

Your life is not defined by parenthood; rather your parenthood is defined by your life. Start to ask yourself how you want that life to feel, not "go." How do you want your home to feel? What thoughts bring you joy of the days in the future of the life with your child? Have fun with your thoughts, use your imagination, and feel good.

Now, don't get me wrong. There will be days that you think you'll pull out your hair. You will have a bad day here and there. Don't stress about them. Put yourself in a place of appreciation that night, trust that it will all look better in the morning, love the fact that you have a bad day here and there for the contrast, to expand to the next idea of what you want. You don't live a life in moaning like so many, it's a bad blip, not a bad week, bad month, bad year. Look at what thought might have been making you feel less than happy, then quickly release it in your mind. Then refocus on what you appreciate, what you dream of, what you have and what you want. If you can't feel good, feel better. Love, love, love, and breathe.

Affirmation

I know that you are feeling the weight of separation sometimes, dear one. I know that occasionally life seems too much. I'm sorry if sometimes my protection seems like restriction. However, there is so much wonder to explore in this world, let's find some different adventure than one that feels off to me. I'm new at this too. Sometimes, I get it mixed up before I make it clear. It is part of our journey together. But what a journey we are having. Let us distract each other. Let us trust in All That Is, and have some fun for fun sake. I love your laugh, I love your passion. You are my Feeling Good place. I could watch your exploration forever.

Who They Really Are

Part Three:
The Toddler Years

Chapter 8

One to two years

Little Interpreter

This age has such a bad reputation and is seen as a time to work through, control as much as possible and a period of developing yourself as the one in charge, teaching your child to listen and behave.

What a misrepresentation of one of the most exciting times for a parent and a child. Yes, this is the birthplace of the relationship you and your child will have for the rest of your lives together. Here is where you start to offer understanding of how the world and universal powers work, and here is where you and your child play, learn and develop together.

The age of the toddler from the first to the third year of their lives is the foundation of a joyful parenthood. Don't waste this time on getting in a knot because your child can be whiny or throws a tantrum (we all feel like having one of those some days).

What's happening in your baby's world

With the first birthday behind you, you will wake up one day soon and wonder what happened to your bundle of joy that lay in your arms, and even your reckless explorer. Yes, your little toddler will still be into exploring every aspect of life; however, he will also be assimilating discoveries differently, making opinions for himself, defining his likes and dislikes and really deciding how he interprets his space in his new physical form. This can lead to some frustration for you as the parent, when suddenly his opinions might clash with yours. However, breathe before you react to what is being presented to you at the moment and see it for what it really is.

Your baby is so excited. Not only has he spent the last few months exploring his own capabilities and surroundings, but suddenly speech, movement and doing things that you do are right around the corner. Could it be possible to walk and talk and play like mom and dad do? How exhilarating! However, as his horizons expand, so does his conquests, and suddenly it seems he's into everything, trying everything out, looking for new things to try and wanting to do everything on his own. But of course he does. When you want to learn something, what's the point of always having someone do it for you? It seems to make so much sense to your little one. But then suddenly, you're stopping him and telling him "no." How very frustrating!

Frustration goes straight to disconnection and so the gap is created.

Up until now, your baby has been used to asking and pretty much being given. Oh, during the exploration stage you might have said no and practiced the art of distraction, but suddenly your little one has his own opinions and ideas. His wants are more defined and specific. They have sparked the desire of it so strongly, that every no seems to go against his very self.

This is an important time. It is often dismissed by people as "The Terrible Twos". But this dismissal creates a world where people feel they have to gain control, deal with the little terrors, fight to teach what is right and wrong… and quite frankly confuse their child completely. They are only expressing Who They Really Are, and in trying to be controlled, they are being muted and separated. Not only that, but parents are missing out on the amazing opportunity of having an amazing time in their child's world of wonder, play and discovery.

Now, I am not suggesting letting them do everything and anything. My goodness, we've all had some experience with a child that is literally out of control, both by his parents and himself, which doesn't make anyone feel good. No, now is the time to create balance for your young one, as well as a small gap between what he wants and how he gets it.

This time contains the introduction of fear into your baby's world. With the introduction of feelings of frustration and separation comes anxiety and being scared. He will have experienced falling and getting hurt, which can create fear of what will happen in the future, and he will be becoming more aware of what's happening in the family, when you are upset, when things are stressed, and that shift in energy will shake him.

It was when our son was 17 months that our beloved dog ran away and never returned. For ages afterwards, our son couldn't sleep alone for any long periods of time and he panicked if we weren't in sight. From that day forward he went from being a part time co-sleeper to full time. He was simply terrified that if one family member could disappear without explanation, then another one could. But since he learned how to talk late, this could only be found out by watching him, tapping into Who He Is and sensing his anxiety when he saw photos of our dog, or looked at pictures of dogs in books. Sometimes, getting to the root of the problem can feel like detective work, but in looking for it, you are acting from the situation rather than reacting to what your child is presenting to you at the moment. After all, when not looking at a child's fear from their perspective, it is easy to see sleeping in their parents' bed as spoiling or "giving in" to a child's whim and whimsy. Fear can come in many forms, from being frightened of the dark or scary dreams, or even odd situations that you might only get a sense of by watching your child get upset without knowing exactly why. Insecurity in someone at this age, especially if they can't talk yet and communication is limited, is a fragile situation and can only be remedied with love, understanding, a lot of hugs and reassurance.

It's also easy to forget that your child is still teething at this point, and they are the bigger teeth near the back which are more painful. Sometimes, the only indicators are fussiness or him bursting into tears at the drop of a hat. This is a big time for your child. Be understanding to that, and trust that giving your child a feeling of security, either by letting him sleep with you, cuddling him for awhile, or using the Art of Distraction will re-establish his feeling good place and the problems will disappear. It feels better than making him stay in his bed no matter what and telling him to just basically get over it. No matter what, it is important, as always, to find yourself a grounded, feeling good place to come from, so you and your child will always be close to your Home. Only from there, will you get a good sense of what is best for your child and how to help him connect to everything he is.

I've noticed that the biggest challenge at the toddler stage is to keep up with their own expansion. They are constantly learning and developing, and looking for more to expand themselves. The minute they get fed up, bored or lose interest in what they know, they leap into wanting to know more. But if that isn't met, they disconnect and lose their balance. It seems to be in that disconnection that fear comes at this age. Also, it is easy for us, as parents, to react to what's being offered to us and misinterpret their disconnection as brattiness or being spoilt. When we get frustrated with them, they disconnect more from Who They Are and it scares them, creating a vicious circle that can only be broken by connecting, and taking our children to the new heights they crave.

Behaviour

If all the world and what we experience is energy, then we use our five senses to interpret that energy. Our own interpretation then forms our opinions, beliefs and personality. During your baby's first year, he was the little explorer, *experiencing* everything within his capacity. However, now after this first birthday, he is truly *interpreting* everything. He is defining it for himself and forming opinions on what he experiences. Therefore, when you tell him No, he can't experience something. His opinion becomes short lived and he gets frustrated and mad. This can lead to crying, screaming, and a tantrum. Of course, the initial shock of this behaviour will send you mad, and then it will snowball into something high in energy, low in efficiency and very disconnected to Source. But there are many ways to stay connected. The first is to understand that your baby isn't intending to get under your skin, he's just following his natural impulses, which is a good thing. The second is, that the tantrum is simply his feelings of frustration regarding the situation coming out, and third, you then flipping out in frustration over his frustration isn't going to help.

What do we know about tantrums? Well, basically it is a flood of emotion, often aimed at the parent who is still the provider and suddenly, the "no sayer." You are still seen as the giver to your baby's asking, so your no feels far off for your baby. Now, tantrums would be a lot more frequent and loud if you hadn't been trying to be a spiritually aware parent up to this point. As it stands, it's simply an expression of contrast. And as that, well, that's something we can all understand.

When your baby is experiencing contrast, see it for what it is. Take a deep breath and see it from his situation. Then pick him up calmly, tell him, in simple terms, why he can't do whatever he's wanting to do. Through the use of facial expressions and small words get the feeling of your meaning across, then move him somewhere and play with him a bit. He might feel a little shaken up the first time this type of severe separation occurs, so go gently. The idea as a spiritually aware parent is not to harden your child to his emotions and to stop feeling. Rather, all you will be looking for over the next few years of his childhood is a more productive way of expressing them. Just as we all do, he needs to learn to express what's frustrating and then move on to a feeling good place. He doesn't like the feelings of lack of control, frustration and upset. He might seem to take a bit of pleasure in sending you round the bend, especially as he gets older, but that isn't mean spirited. Rather, it's just another step of exploration. However, as he currently lacks the communication skills to express how he is feeling, it can be incredibly frustrating for him and easy to misread what he's going through.

I can't express more how important it is to talk to your child, to communicate with your child. We have always used a wide gamut of ways of expressing how we feel, and I'm happy to say our children were able to express themselves, even without words, from an early age. Even though at the toddler stage, they can't communicate what they are thinking or wanting to express, the power of comprehension of this age always surprises me. If a child is used to being talked to, and talked to properly, not just baby talk, then by the age of 18 months many children will be able to understand concepts like "Let's go upstairs," "Let's do a puzzle," "Would you like to watch a movie?" as well as more complicated and abstract ideas. To enable your child to understand your meaning from an early age will mean he understands *why* you say no, rather than seeing it as a random act of cruelty for no reason. Use words, sounds, and facial expressions to help your child learn how to express his emotions and how he feels. Be consistent in their use and use them when any similar situations come up. Your child will quickly have a deep understanding of how the feeling place works. It will also help him recognize that all living things function on a feeling place/spirit level. With this in place, tantrums are avoided simply by using a simple phrase and then distracting your child onto something else.

In this foundational stage of communication with your child, take into consideration the words you use and the intention you use them with. During your baby's first year, he was fascinating to watch and the temptation to criticize his explorations or use terms like "bad" or "naughty" seemed impossible, but now as he moves into more determined exploring and a seeking of independence, in *off* moments you might get tempted to let negative words slip. As a parent, it's always felt incredibly *off* for me to use the phrases "bad boy" or "bad girl." If you have to use the term bad, then I usually try to make the distinction between calling an action bad versus the child. I feel that calling someone bad can do serious damage by preventing them from trusting their inner guidance system, and most of the time, even if they aren't doing what we want them to do, they are in fact following what they feel is alright. Often things will feel better if you just distract your child from the situation, or point out how you are dealing with it instead.

Words can hurt and even if you don't think your child can understand the words, from infancy they can read the intention behind them, even if it's just the casual use of "darling" or "sweetie" versus "rascal," "little monster" or "holy terror."

As important as it is to use this type of emotional communication when your child is doing something you wish he wouldn't, it is also vital to use it when he is doing something that is wonderful in your eyes, or even when you are showing him something great. Showing your enthusiasm over something he is doing, showing your appreciation for a thing of beauty, or showing your delight in your food, all of this leads to more for your child to explore and understand. That's not to say go overboard, or try to feel something you don't instinctually feel. Your baby is still reading your feelings not your words and the contradicting vibration you are emitting will only confuse him. Stay connected, stay true to how you feel, and let your baby do the same.

You are an example for your child. If you shout, your child will shout. If you criticize, your child will too. If you praise your child, he will be more likely to praise and feel greater contrast within himself when he doesn't.

However, there is a flip side to the topic of communication and that is listening to your child, even before his language is fully developed. It is not uncommon for a child to still not talk by the age of three. However, as most parents know, a child is fully capable of getting his point across. The more attentive you are to what he's trying to express to you, the more positive this communication will be, and by using words to respond to him, you will be showing him that you are listening and he doesn't have to worry he won't be heard. It can be heart lifting to watch a young child of this age come up with ways to explain what they want to express. From bringing toys to the TV to show what they want to watch, to pointing to photographs or using sign; the eagerness to express themselves is wonderful. It doesn't mean you have to give your child whatever they ask for, however they ask for it. Even manners can be introduced before language, simply by teaching them to not grab from you, but ask with a kiss or an open hand and introducing the idea of them having to wait a moment to get it. Therefore, stay alert and attentive. If your child is going to this effort to express something to you, he will have a foundation of being listened to whenever you notice them. If you get tempted to brush it off and tell him to be quiet, then he will feel alone, helpless and suddenly suppressed. Merely contrast for your developing little one, but not a good foundation for feeling good for either one of you, and that is the point after all.

Ah yes, feeling good, or as I like to say Jiving. At this point in your child's experience it is still easy to see whether they are connected or not, but suddenly it becomes from the way he jives, his eyes dance and sparkle, he laughs with a great belly laugh, he comes up with games and dances about. As a parent, I like to keep our children in this state as much as possible, mainly because it's so much more fun. From a jiving point, they never cry, never fuss or whine, and they are just so much fun to play with. When a child is jiving, and feeling good, life is easy and it is the pinnacle of parenthood.

But, let's face it, they don't jive all the time, and like I mentioned before, a fit of teething, a fall, a scary dream, even a sense of tension can throw them out of their feeling good space. That's life and that's the contrast that makes us all grow and expand. There are some days where you wonder why your child is a totally different person, and then the next morning or some morning soon, they're back. The important thing in all of this is to stay in the feeling good zone yourself. Don't react to your child's temporary *off*-ness. When we let how we feel be governed by how our children behave, we are telling them that our happiness depends on them and what they do. Even from this young age, that is too much to carry. These are foundational years, and in the toddler years a parent's happiness can be put to the test. Therefore, take a moment every once in a while through the day to stop and check in with yourself. Breathe, appreciate and look around you. And remind yourself that your child is experiencing an off day. See if you can spark something to call him back to himself and to feel good again. Rather than rushing him off to bed to get the day over with, sit with him, read to him, play with him. Even chase him round the room and tickle him to make him laugh. He will feel the relief of feeling good again and go to bed happy and you will see your angel sleeping and not feel like you missed an opportunity to help him feel more himself. It never takes much to make a child laugh, even a funny face, and to get them used to the idea of the phenomenal relief one feels when they let go and feel good helps them the rest of their lives.

As we know, throughout life we are constantly asking. We ask for things, for improved circumstances, for better treatment, for freedom, for time, anything that the human mind can imagine. Spirit hears these requests, and moves to the achievement of them. All we have to do is keep up by getting connected, feeling good, and into the feeling space of what we want. Often we just keep asking, staying in the same place asking away, which makes us feel miserable and disconnected. It's only by finding that jiving point that the Law of Attraction can offer a different circumstance.

As parents, we're in an interesting place with our toddlers. We are like the universe for them for those first years. In the beginning we provided everything with ease and our little ones kept connected most of the time. They then started exploring, but were happy in all exploration so all we had to do was provide the venue. Suddenly the toddler stage brings a lot more contrast. They want more specific things. They want intangible things such as to be understood, to be able to communicate better, to be able to touch what you touch etc. When they can't have a quick achievement of that, they disconnect and it feels awful to them. A tantrum follows, understandably, and a parent is left wondering what to do. From a spiritual point, it is a harsh choice to punish a tantrum, as really it's teaching a child to not follow their gut instincts, to feel what they feel, and rather it tells them they have to behave exactly how you wish in order to be acceptable behaviour. However, giving into a tantrum doesn't work either. If we provide, as the universe provides, for our toddlers, theoretically it would be good practice to only provide when they are jiving and feeling connected. If they are disconnected, feeling miserable and kicking on the floor, they would never attract from the universe what they wanted; therefore, it would be a mixed message to get it from us. Also, no matter what, it hardly ever feels good to us to give in at that place. Now saying that, the only choice then is to use the Art of Distraction, find anything and everything to distract, get them jiving and then reconsider if they can achieve what they wanted.

A toddler's distraction is different from his earlier ones. Literally as the parent, you have to become the kid inside of yours. You have to use great imaginational force and distract away. Putting things in boxes, floating things in puddles, trying to fit a rope through a small hole, drawing attention to the little things at this age is a brilliant way of distracting your young toddler, and refocusing him away from the dangerous. Also, when he is jiving again with his new discovery, he's achieved a certain amount of what he's been asking for, even if it's just by being interested in something or being amused. After he's jiving again, consider what he wanted before. Will it expand his experience, or will it go unnoticed. Of course, most of the things we refuse are because they're dangerous, so if that's the case, while he's refocused on the distraction you provided, hide the danger away somewhere and all will continue to be blissful.

I find at this stage, it's important to create fun and toddler-type things and to really get into the groove of being one or two years old. Have fun with it and enjoy the fascinating world through the eyes of a child. Then, call your toddler over and show him something amazing, like putting lids on jars or dirt in a bucket. If I call our son over to see something entertaining, I find he is more likely to take notice of me in other circumstances too. It stops me from becoming something that stops him from having fun and turns me into a fun creator, who occasionally offers something other than what he was looking for, but ends with the same result.

This is true with universal powers too. Often we think we have a plan, an idea of how we want things to go down to the last detail. But when we release it to a higher power, and enjoy our now, that power delivers something of equal or greater bliss and our plans pale in comparison to the new situation we find ourselves in.

It is important to remember that as a spiritually aware parent, who is trying (although it is hard to all the time) to see your child as Pure, Positive Energy, and to help keep him connected to Who He Really Is as often as possible, it is important at this stage not to use terms like "control" or "mould" in your speech or even in your thoughts. Once again, I'm not encouraging the practice of letting your child be "free" and fall down the stairs and break his neck. Rather, I'm talking about letting these words enter at their meaning state. To control someone is to let their inner voice bend to yours. And although it is a good thing to pick up a child in danger or to decide a child is too tired to continue with his day, it is easy to decide that you will control all elements of their experience, which you can't. At this age it might seem that you can, but it is important to let your child form his own opinions and not hear it from you first.

With our first two children, I made the mistake of starting to use guilt. If they did something nasty, I made it seem worse. I fed the feeling of disappointment. I tried to control the situation. When I started to realize how *off* this felt, to all of us, I changed direction. Talking and talking and talking NEVER works. Please take it from me. Rather, pick your battles and be quick and direct. If your child is putting something in his mouth which is dangerous, choose to control. But give your child the feeling of creating his own opinions by giving him occasional options. Even letting him choose to try different fruit, or pick toys and books, will give him the chance to make his own mind. This means his opinion matters, and he has a say. Even at this young age, I was asking our children to see which pair of shoes they swayed towards or which biscuits to buy. I remember being hassled by a woman in a shop once, who told me, "Don't ever give them options." As if to say, "You'll never be able to control them then." I also remember how it would feel so *off* to not let our children have some influence in the little things. Now, I would suggest giving only a couple, maybe three choices, as it can be too overwhelming. I also suggest avoiding your own frustration by making sure you give choices that don't matter to you. Wait, that's worth repeating.

Give choices, but only for things that don't matter to you! You don't want to ask "Do you want to go to bed now?" to your 18-month old, just as "Should we go out today?" will be too big of a question to him too. But choice can make your child feel that he can like something different, can make a choice and take part in things as a family. So, keep it for the little things, even asking what t-shirt he should wear, or which toy to bring out.

The word "mold" is very much the same thing, but the intention when you use it seems different. Whereas control means to keep your child under your thumb and suppress him, mould means to make a mini You. Either one is stressful, upstream, denying your child's true self, and impossible no matter how hard you would try. So, acknowledge your child as his own spirit, who you are trying to give the tools to feel good to, and then make him feel good. Letting go a little bit of how he turns out will make you feel good too.

Your baby is constantly watching you and others around him, and interpreting it through his senses. At this age he is eager to make the connection that whatever you can do he can do too. Therefore, he is constantly mimicking and copying your actions. That is why it is so frustrating for him when you say no. However, the simple tasks of establishing whose things are whose will help in this. Find similar items to what you use for your child. Toy tools, pots and pans etc. being his to use while you use the real things will tide him over until you can teach him how to help you do a few easy tasks. When he is two, there might be a few things he can even help with, such as filling up a pet's dish, or watering some plants. Even at a year, a child can hold something and help carry things. Whenever I'm holding our son and I go to the fridge, I always let him carry one thing for me, such as jam or cheese. He's also eager to put the sweepings from the dustpan into the garbage, or put laundry in the hamper. He's always so proud of it. When he can't actually help, finding alternatives can be a fun distraction, and provide you with heart-explosive pride. One of my favourites was when our son wanted to help make the morning pancakes, but was happy with the alternative of making his own bowl of cereal, simply by me giving his dry cereal in a bowl, a cup of milk to pour in and a small bit of sugar on the spoon, all from the safety of his highchair. He mixed it all together and was so proud of himself, he ate it all! Mimicking is great fun for your toddler, who will revel in the idea of following in your footsteps. When you actually let him try things out, his exploration expands again, and he is filled to the brim with satisfaction.

Allowing a toddler to "help" fulfills what he is actually trying to do in all of his interpreting. To then receive praise afterwards, rather than to be told yet another "no", is pure bliss for him.

Routine

Although our girls were determined not to nap during the day (their passion for exploration was a full-day experience) I now know that a daily drop-time is a good idea. Now, true this might not actually lead to a full-blown, dream-filled nap; however, if you can find a structure in your day that means you can have some quiet time with your child, it will give good dynamics to your day and refocus both of you back to Source. Sleep is reconnection back to Source; therefore, it brings you back to everything You Really Are. However, don't make it a painful demand. Rather, let your child be quiet. Read some books, play some quiet games, look at things that bring joy. Take a break from any contrast and any possible frustration. Let your little one take a break from exploration and just have some quality time. Chances are, if your child has had a full morning, the quiet drop will lead to some sort of sleep, but don't be stressed if it doesn't.

As your baby moves to more and more proper meals, you will find a true sense of routine. This routine will be in place for a few years. Finally, you can sigh, you have some sort of structure. Your child will get hungry and tired at the same time every day and suddenly this does seem to relieve stress and make everything run more pleasantly. However, don't be surprised if still things beyond your control can switch your routine around.

Even something as simple as the weather, which we take for granted, can alter how our children are feeling, their connection and their state of happiness. For two of our children now, we have noticed that they shone with happiness and contentment when the sun was out, but were also less likely to nap (I guess the sun made them feel so connected, reconnecting to Source was already achieved). However, they were cranky and tired on cloudy, rainy days. To the point that we would dread it when we saw the grey sky, even if it did mean a nap for our daughters was more possible. Watch your child's reaction to the weather of the day and try to be understanding. Once your child can walk, make the grey skies fun by showing him how to splash or float things in puddles, also even a walk in the rain can be interesting or playing with the water in buckets, provided he's not going to drink it. Also, be understanding on cloudy days and see if it matches with your baby's mood. If it is, go gently, make him laugh and spend some quality time creating inner sunshine. Routines can always be picked up again the next day.

At this time there may be another shift in your baby's routine. Whereas it is the common practice to either breastfeed or bottlefeed your baby into a blissful slumber, now you may be heading into the time of actually putting your child to sleep. Start this off before you've actually weaned and it will be an easier transition. Take about half an hour and have some true quality time with your child. Read him some stories, watch something quiet (The baby Einstein videos are perfect or Classical baby). Listen to some music. Have a specific wind-down period, so that your child gets lulled to a calm state. If he falls asleep, that's alright, or simply move him to his bed (or yours, if that may be the case) and let him finally drift there. You might also try some calming atmosphere, such as candles, or incense depending on what is possible and relaxing in your home. No matter how you do it, make sure you take advantage of this calm time. Through the day, the daily rituals can go by without true connection between you two, now savour it. It is sweet bliss to sit with your child, setting all other things aside, and lull him into a deep calm before sleep.

Health and nutrition

The spiritual connection to food is as natural as eating itself. We appreciate everything we eat, and it is even better when you take part in natural food that is full of obvious goodness. You can often even feel it feeding every one of your cells and organs. Your baby feels this too and responds best to natural foods. However, as we discussed in the last section, this can often be hard to find.

I want to bring your attention to the anti-spiritual affect of food colourings. Although I'm sure you aren't handing your one or two year old candy, which with its coloured stripes and spots screams artificial food colourings, it is often hard to get away from these in other sources. It is worth checking lists of ingredients for these and artificial sweeteners as they can literally take your grounded and happy child and send him wild. Suddenly, after consuming these (especially the yellow colouring tartrazine), your child will start to act faster, talk higher and go through crazy mood swings of being totally happy (but in a hyper, not jiving, way) to a total wreck. It is my belief that if children diagnosed with Attention Deficiency Disorder cut out food colourings entirely from their diet, they would be fine within a very short period of time. However, it is also sometimes hard to believe where these culprits lie. Where we live, even butter is sometimes coloured with yellow food dye, as are many pops, juices, and pre-made dinners such as macaroni or curries, or desserts like custard or sponge cakes (or medications if you decide to use any for cold and flus. The worst culprit of this I've found is both artificial colour and sweeteners in teething gel!). Sometimes, as our children have reacted to this, we find ourselves getting upset or aggravated only to find that really they aren't at fault at all. This was probably one of the spearheads of really looking at spiritual parenting as getting cross can never feel good as a parent, but getting cross only to find out it's a chemical reaction in your child is even worse!

Due to the age of your child, I would suggest cutting all colourings as much as possible. Already, your child is experiencing the emotional ups and downs of exploring and learning new things, this sort of artificial influences amplifies them and you'll end up thinking you're raising a brat. You aren't.

Now, in many countries and products, work is being done to cut out artificial colourings and use natural ones instead. This is often labelled on the ingredients listings. It is worth taking the time to read and find out.

Drawing on what was discussed earlier about choices, let your child form his own ideas about what he likes in the food category and what he doesn't. Vegetables and fruits, which are so important to a healthy diet, have such a broad range that even if your child doesn't like his cabbage, he very well might like his kale or green beans. By the time your child is two you can probably start explaining to him that vegetables are needed to help his body work. Our girls had been taught the colour green by this age and told that they had to have at least one thing green every day. But let your child have his own opinion about the good food he likes. Nothing sets up a bad relationship with food than being forced to eat something you hate because it's "good for you." It leads to rebellion in future years and makes it about power. Start now in helping your child make healthy choices. Provide a variety of fruits and vegetables, start exploring as a family. Your little one will happily jump on board.

Meditation and back to Source

Ah, I always breathe a sigh of relief when getting to this section and the reason is the perfect focus for your child at this stage. It is so nice to focus on what feels good rather than what feels *off*. Yet, for some bizarre reason, it is easy as a parent to focus on what is going wrong, or crazy, or what feels stressful in your day with your child. To be spiritually aware is to find appreciation in everything and in anything and to pass this on to your child. At this stage, your child is moving about, reading the energy of everything and interpreting it for himself. Therefore, let him know now about the energy of a quiet head and a happy heart. When he is busy at something, rather than doing chores or getting something done, sit near him and just breathe and appreciate. Raise the feeling that vibrates from you. Look for anything you can to appreciate and really let it settle in you to make you feel good. If you want, find other things that make you joy-full. Bring yourself to that place of peaceful exhilaration. Sitting cross legged on the floor, maybe with candles or incense if they make you feel at ease, sit your child on your lap and let him experience this calm. Look at some pretty pictures, watch the candles (safely) float and dance about. Focus on anything that inspires calm, even if it only lasts five minutes. Even if it only lasts two! When your child gets restless, put him somewhere safe and continue soaking it up yourself. Start to be the example. Your child will sense you feeling happy, he will see it calms you and makes you brighter. He will see the change in you and instinctually you will pass on the idea of calm, of quiet and joyful peace.

Also, although it seems your child is ready to run and explore 24/7, take time to just connect with him sitting down in a quiet space. Look into each other's eyes, play some games, read some books or simply chatter. Take sanction in each other's smiles and know that you love each other. Sometimes, there is nothing that puts me in a better feeling good place, a place of well-being and spiritual groundedness, than connecting to everything our children Really Are. Looking at them as Who They Really Are, and connecting to that, even simply making him laugh will make your day so much brighter, for both of you.

Fun and games

Your child understands magic at its deepest level and at this point in his life he doesn't need to only believe it exists in an unseen realm; rather, he feels it in everything around him. This is definitely the age of wonder, and it is eye-opening for you as a parent to follow suit and really explore the world from this magical perspective.

As your child is using his senses to read and interpret the energy of things around him, support that by encouraging him to use every one of his senses to explore different things. For instance;

Smell - Show him how to breathe in deeply and smell. Let him smell flowers, spices, baking, food, herbs. Talk to him about the smell too. If you smell something bad, then sniff up and express yourself. Maybe, he'll form a different opinion or maybe the same. I mean, out of our family, my husband and I like the smell of skunk, where our daughters don't at all.

Touch - Re-awaken a sensitive touch when it comes to the feel of things. Pat animals or stuffed toys. Stroke ribbons, velvets or smooth leather on shoes. Run his hand through water, play with sand. If you notice he's interested in something you're wearing, then feel it with him. Our daughters used to always love to rub their hands over a velvet skirt of mine, whereas I have specific memories of playing with a tassel on one of my mother's necklaces. There are also a lot of great board books with various textures in them to start this exploration of touch.

Sight - Point out everything. Birds, trees, cars, trains, plants, grass. Read to your child, not necessarily the words, but point out images he might recognize and say the names. Also, point out people, especially those in his family. At about one, I gave our daughter a photo album of her own and it was filled with photos of her and members of her family, including grandparents, aunts and uncles. We would go through it and say the names together. It got completely crumpled over time, but she was fascinated. We also love taking our children out after dark and showing them the stars and moon. Since the first time we showed the moon to our son, he is constantly looking out of windows after dark and a quick point to the night sky tells me to sing "I see the Moon" as his lullaby at night. It's a magical thing to see the world transform after dusk. Actually, make them marvel even more and show them a sunset.

Taste - Explore tastes through a variety of food. Let your baby really try things out and form his own opinion. Of course in many ways, he's been exploring through this sense ever since he got the craving to start sticking everything in his mouth.

Hearing - There is something that is so profound to think that hearing was the first sense your child started to explore energy with, all the way back to when he was in your womb. Draw to his attention the various sounds around. Birds are wonderful for this, especially if you can spot where it actually is and see him making his call. Listen for the trickle of water, or even the sound of the bath running. Listen for animal sounds, such as a dog barking or a cat. Use gentle sounds as much as possible, the undertones of a cricket rather than the jolting wail of a fire engine. Start to pull your child's attention to the silence as well. So often, we are bombarded by noise, whereas the undertones of the world can bring us back to ourselves.

It is the little bits of wonder that can be fun at this age. Taking pleasure in things like rainbows and flowers can slow your little one down and make magic for both of you. Pick up a few prism crystals and hang them in the window of a room your child spends a lot of time in during the time when the sun pours through the window. When it does, have fun with the rainbows shining on the wall. Spin the crystal about and watch them dance about. As your child gets closer to the two-year mark, let him chase the rainbows; talk about the colours and enjoy the magic together.

A garden is a wonderful thing to start with your child. At about 18 months your child can fill pots up with soil and even push seeds into it. Give him a watering can and let him help water them and watch them grow. I must admit we've been parents who've encouraged a great relationship with soil for our children, and they have no problems getting their hands dirty (or their legs, faces, and whole selves). Watching them thrill at each discovery in the soil, every new plant, small worm, and stones, have brought so much joy to our family. Their explorations have expanded over the years, but this initial age really gets them on their feet running when it comes to play.

The key to games at this age is quick turn over and knowing when to make the shift. This comes in two ways. First, when your child is being really, really active, be it if he's running all over the room as you run after him, or if he's playing peek-a-boo behind something, or he's just laughing so hard he can't stop, you can ride the wave to keep things going well, and slow it down a bit before he loses control and hurts himself. Our son loves to run around the bed when I'm getting him dressed. I jump on the bed to surprise him on the other side, or play peek-a-boo from one end when he's at the other. However, after about 10 minutes, I'm worn out, and I know it could start to feel *off* to me soon. Also, he starts to run the risk of getting hurt. So usually, I will quickly sit on the bed, grab one of his books and call him over to read it or I'll mention a family member's name and tell him we should go see what they're doing. He'll happily stop the chase, slow down, get dressed and we continue enjoying each other's company.

The other way that sensing when your child is ready for a shift is a little more subtle. It comes when a child has grown so used to his usual life that he feels stuck. We'll talk about it more in the following book for older children, but in this toddler stage, they show this feeling of stagnancy by becoming aimless. It comes quickly. One day they will be happy playing with blocks or a pull toy, the next day they never even look at them and they are into everything you've tried to steer them away from (our little boy has a fondness for putting the cat food into the cat's water and then putting it on the floor in various places when he's fed up). It also might be marked by your child getting sick more, or getting upset more often. Yet, often it doesn't take very much for a complete haul over of playthings and surroundings to fix it up perfectly. I made the mistake with our daughters of bringing some toys out too soon, so by the time they were ready for them they were so used to seeing them around they never looked twice at them. But with our son, I try to keep a few tricks up my sleeve. His 8x4 playpen has had numerous changes and all spearheaded by signs he was getting disconnected from disinterest. The overhauls usually mean getting rid of some things he never looks at, some he has grown out of, and then adding and organizing some older and definitely new-to-him toys and game ideas. It works every time and each time I do it, he spends all his time in a place he wouldn't step foot in before.

Toys and products

Somewhere between the one and two-year mark toys and things move from adding further exploration for your child to introducing and encouraging creativity in your child. Creativity is really an extension of exploration for everyone, really. It's just further exploring Who You Really Are and your personal inner world. Art and crafts are expressions of that world. Now, your one or two year old isn't really ready for true art. It's not really necessary, as they are more focused on expressing opinions in this world, rather than exploring inner worlds. That can wait for a couple more years. However, by 18 months, chunky crayons and paper are a fun distraction from the pens you use. This is when remembering that your child wants to copy your actions comes in handy. I remember our daughters always wanting to write as we did and they would get to the pens. Every important document I had seemed to have a scribble on it by one of them. However, making sure they know your pens are yours, and then supplying them with an alternative that is theirs is a good way round it.

Watch for things your child is mimicking you with and provide toy alternatives. Toy kitchens and utensils, toy tools, toy cars, whatever you see sparking interest.

I'm not hung up on the effects of dolls and playhouses on a boy. It always strikes me unfair that girls can like blue, build with tools, and play with cars, but boys can't like pink, play with dolls or play house. This kind of action man based providing seems to lead to the result of males being forced to hide their emotions and act tough, which of course means they aren't listening to their emotional guidance system and cutting themselves off. I'm not saying that I feel comfortable giving a frilly, pink-laced baby doll to our son, but more for the fact, I don't think he would like it, anyway there are plenty of boyish dolls out there. If you feel he would enjoy something like it and he would be using his mimicking skills, then do it. From an early age a child can pretend to feed a toy and put it to sleep and this continues his exploration of doing things you do.

There is a division at this time between the age when everything is going into his mouth and when its not. Suddenly, this will stop being the automatic reaction when something new comes his way, and he'll use other senses to explore rather than just taste. Hold off on a lot of stuff before this ends. Playdough and crayons, and anything not really… well tasty, can wait until he will really appreciate them.

Paddling pools and sand boxes (once he stops putting everything in his mouth) are also a must. Outside play makes a break from the house and redirects the constant explorations that have been happening indoors.

Reading with your toddler is a great experience if you haven't already started in their baby years, and at this time I also like to bring out chunky puzzles, blocks to build towers with and knock them down and a few things to push about. I like to find a balance of things that I can do along with our child, and show him how to do new things, as well as things he can then amuse himself with. Usually, I find that the things I buy at this age are for us both to quietly sit and do, whereas on his own, our son would be happiest with two cups and water to pour back and forth between them.

Holidays

Right now, your child is perfectly happy living his day to day life adventure. However, it's a great time for you to start to experiment with how you feel about each holiday you feel compelled to celebrate. Social pressure, even consumer pressure, can make holidays and traditions seem so forced and so far from yourself. Agree with everyone involved with your family celebrations that, due to your child's age, you want to be a little bit liberated from the pressures of it all. Then start looking at what you love about each holiday, what really makes you jive? Then try forming new traditions to really take advantage of this. Holidays are meant to be fun, not about have to's. So, relax and have fun, and take note from your child; do some exploration and figure out your opinions, beliefs and personal interpretations.

Test a few things out when you decide which holidays mean something to you and how you want to pass them on to your children. Traditions can be started with you as well as passed on from your family experiences. Take the ones from your past that you feel good about, then totally change around the stuff that has always felt *off* to you.

Stay aware of the fact that holidays can really throw your child out of feeling good. Between everyone getting excited, stressed and anxious, to visitors and strangers coming around, to bringing a tree into the living room, there's a lot that your toddler will feel uncertain about. What's worse is that often we parents suddenly have a lot of things to do and spending time reading books together or playing take backburner which leaves our children asking why. Therefore, be easy on them. Keep the routines of the day as normal as possible. Keep naptimes, mealtimes and whatever other times intact and don't believe your child has to have every traditional experience within the first couple of years of birth. Also, enjoy the experience of this year, when with children things change so rapidly.

One Christmas, when our daughters were seven and eight and our son only 18 months, I was worried about how the morning traditions would go. Images of our son learning about wrapped presents and tearing the paper off no matter whose worried me. I soon regained a feeling good position and marveled at how our son dealt with it all. His sisters showed him how to open gift-wrap, but after I gave him his first (a board book) he never looked for another; he just sat there "reading". He got fed up sooner or later and then we brought out another present for him, moving slowly, and with confusion on his face, he happily opened his lot and played all day with the girls. I did find that playing some of his normal activities, and making sure he had his normal nap was important, so that the sense of a totally new adventure wasn't too overwhelming, and it became just a routine day with presents and family time to boot.

Try to use New Year's as a reset button. Use it to look back at your year and to figure out what's working well and what's not? How is your home feeling? Is there stress or does it burble with joy? Are you getting enough time with a quiet head or is everything loud and frantic until you go to bed? Looking at New Year's as a time of rebooting your spiritual groundedness and feeling good makes New Year's resolutions something to really get excited about. It's a bench mark to start fresh, make a few shifts and get back into the joy of things.

Who They Really Are

*You as parent, you as **YOU***

Your child is building his own inner world and already his personality is separated from you. If you were breastfeeding, this might be coming to an end and you are making the shift to a different sort of dependency your child has on you. Embrace the time you've had, and make a conscious shift. Remember the time that's been. Make a photo album or even an inspiration board of your time in babydom and embrace the child that now stands on his own before you.

Take time to establish who you are as a parent and what you've observed in yourself so far. What brings you joy and what bugs you? Are you someone who gets joy out of their child looking clean and neat or are you willing to let that go? Do piercing screams and whines drive you mad or do you feel it is done in play so get joy out of it? There are no right answers. You can't get it wrong. It is all just expressions of Who You Really Are. Staying true to these observations gives the clearest experience of that and also gives your child the experience of who they choose as a parent.

So, what about your home? Are you happy with how it feels on an energy level? Does it give you relief when you walk through the door after being out? Do you wake up happy to be where you are?

Now is a great time to start to look at the undertones of your house. By undertones I mean the essence of your home, the vibrational bottom line. The undertone is what lies underneath and what we all resort to. This can be one of contentment, satisfaction or happiness. It can jive with the exhilaration of everyone in the family constantly growing and learning. It can also sometimes have an undertone of fear, frustration, bitterness or resentment if things are being left unresolved or happy face stickers are being put over things that are bothering you. Now that you are more than one, now that you are a family unit, the undertone as a whole can act as a point for The Law Of Attraction as strongly as your own individual feeling place. Now, I'm not saying to make serious changes if you feel that another person in the family is affecting the undertone; that's not going to help it at all. Rather, make a conscious effort to decide what you want the undertone of your home to be, and basically Be It. Everyone else will follow suit, and what's even more exciting is that it's like a vibrational soup pot. You will offer your feeling place, and then your partner will offer theirs, and then your children will offer theirs. If you've talked about wanting a certain kind of home and everyone starts to offer a respectful, appreciative and loving vibration to your home, your undertone will have people feeling so much better after visiting you and your family, you will feel happy and content when you are at home and your house will simply ring with laughter and kind words.

Are you happy? I don't mean all the time, for contrast keeps us ever expanding and that means you have to have some not so good days, but on the whole. Do you find it easy to jump into an appreciation rant?

As you're child pasts his second milestone, you will find more and more time with your thoughts and dreams. Take this time to reboot yourself. Appreciate where you are, focus on all the positive, wonder-full things in your life and in your world and then start looking at the more. Not taking any of the shine off of your Now, start to look forward to where you are going. Do you have dreams? Desires? Take some time to empower them. They might have changed since another soul has entered your life, or you might still jive at some thought that has driven you for a long time. Let whatever stirs you fill you up once in awhile. You know now how fast time flies, and as an example for your child, reassure yourself that you can do anything and that everything is possible.

Check to see what your default is. What is the feeling place you spend the most time in? What is the one you drop into during your day-to-day living? Is it a conscious default or do you usually go about your activities being mostly unaware of how you feel until you draw your attention back to it? Although it is easy to say Feel Good, it takes mental practice and true commitment to steer your mind and retrain it from letting the negative thoughts coming in. It seems that in the world of today, frustration, anger, resentment even boredom are seen as the normal way of life, and to be happy as you walk down the street earns you odd looks from passers-by. So, what's your default and what do you want it to be?

If there are days when it feels like your feeling place should drop down in the priority list, trust me, sit and appreciate and raise the vibration of how you feel and make yourself feel better. When you are feeling good and feeling connected to Who You Really Are, your parenting tools go through the roof. Now, as I said in the baby section, I'm not encouraging anyone to shut the baby out and do anything or say anything to get some time alone. I'll say it again, you can't feel good from being nasty or aggravated, irritated or frustrated. You simply can't make that leap. It never feels deeply good to feel that situations, circumstances or even people have to change in order for you to feel better. Rather, feel good in whatever life is bringing forth your way. When your child is napping, or has just gone to bed, when he's safely playing in a playpen, or even if you hand him over to a family member while you find the space you need, FEEL GOOD!

How does it affect your parenting you may wonder? In every way. You'll be more on top of falls and bumps from your baby. Your instincts will become razor-sharp. You'll be able to understand your child's desires and needs on a deeper level beyond communication. You'll know the right thing to say and when to say it. You'll be present for your child, in the moment and in your body rather than having a billion things in your brain at once and making your child feel the distance. As your child grows, you will become the example of how to deal with other people, listening to your own heart and following the indicators from how you feel. Also, as your child grows older, and his asking turns to more physical things, such as toys at stores, candy, special treats or playing with friends, you will have a 24-hour guide within you that you can rely on. At anytime your child asks for anything, you can drop into that feeling good space and see if it feels good to grant the wish or if it feels *off*. If it does, you will have the confidence to be able to say no, backed up simply with "It doesn't feel right to me." What an example for your child to witness. And what a tool for your child to grow up with, to be able to confidently tell his peers when he is older that he won't do something as it feels *off* from Who He Really Is.

Therefore, take some time, even if it's just before you go to sleep, to refocus on feeling good and trust that the better you feel, the better all things will be. With a little bit of effort and a bit of practice, you will be able to shift your perspective around a few times to find a feeling good thought about anything. This is by far the most powerful key to being a spiritually aware parent. For by getting into the practice of this now, you are paving the way of your parenting for the future. You are establishing a magical relationship with your child, keeping him as Pure Positive Energy in your eyes and understanding, enjoying and feeling good about his exploration, his passion, his curiosity and his zest for life. By feeling good now, you make your child's life feel good and you create a happy home. Isn't that a reason to practice thinking and feeling good…NOW?

A guide to being a spiritually aware parent

<u>Affirmation</u>

There are so many changes in your experience, dear one. Suddenly, you seem to grow and want more so quickly. I love your passion. I love your drive. I dislike the feeling of restricting you. Sometimes, it seems like what I want and what you want are different things. But it's not true. We both want to experience, but we see it from different perspectives. We are like a coin, with two sides. But I will trust in the inner workings of us both. I will trust my feeling place, and if something feels off, I will tell you it cannot be. However, when something feels off to you, it too cannot be. We will Feel Good together, from different sides, but of the same coin.

Who They Really Are

A guide to being a spiritually aware parent

Final Thoughts

As you move towards your child hitting the magic age of two, I would like to suggest a philosophy for you to ponder.

All of us are pure positive spiritual beings at our core. We are eternal spirits, who experience the time in these bodies in order to have contrast, which results in desire, which then results in the creation of eternal more, more of everything, especially more new ideas and new expansion. Death is simply re-emergence into non-physical. And in being non-physical, we still crave expansion and still experience the rush of the new idea. We then become physical again, choosing the new time as it has all the expansion that's gone before behind it.

When we connect to our spirit, our soul, source or God, we have access to all the expansion and the new ideas that have gone before. We are not content with learning or regurgitating the same old things that have been said and taught for years. Rather, we crave to take that further.

Does this not put a different slant on what we call the generation gap or evolution? As parents, we often feel we can't control our kids or stop them from rolling their eyes at us as they hit teenage years. However, if our children are the next generation, the new evolved beings, then it is backwards for us to try to make them conform to the old idea. Rather, it is vital for them to feel empowered to trust their own connection to Source, to look to what feels good at their core and stirs them to joy and further expansion. This is not to say that they know more than us, although as they progress through to adult hood this might be the case. Rather it is part of our expansion to help them realize theirs.

We are all in this together. Your expansion, your new ideas, your passions, joys and thrills are the keys to your journey here on Earth. Therefore, pursuing those is actually key to being a spiritually aware parent. Through example, through living your words and to your pinnacle, you inspire your child to not be a mini-you but to live to their pinnacle: generation after generation after generation, each one becoming the new leading edge of thought and joy. What a thing to take part in.

At this point in your child's life this concept won't be a readily useable tool. Rather I find it simply an interesting undertone to how you deal with your child throughout his life. He is a wise, living spirit, who has come here to enjoy this life with you. You chose this life long before, just as he did, yet now you are truly connected together. Therefore, rather than teaching him to look at life as how it is, pass on to him the magic of seeing how life could be. Together, let us take thought, expansion and joyful experience to a whole new level.

With every bad day, every good day, every connection and every disconnection, we are expanding. Have fun in this thing called parenthood. It is a blissful way of expanding and learning about yourself.

Now saying that, with everything you've read in this book, take from it what you like and leave out the rest. Through your own expansion, add what you like and no matter what, do what

A guide to being a spiritually aware parent

feels good to you. For when you feel good you are connected to everything You Really Are. You are connected to a mine of wisdom and good direction. When you feel good, you are connected to Source, and from there only the best of inspired action will follow. Make it your mission to do anything and everything it takes to find yourself a good feeling thought place and know that you will know the right course to take.

Trust me when I say, "You are doing exceptionally well."

Notes On This Second Edition

When I was little being "grown up" implied that my growing would be done. One day, I thought, I would wake up and be complete, the transition would be made and I would be fully myself, to enjoy the rest of life as the person I had become. However, I didn't realize that life is never stagnant. As humans we are forever growing and learning, as I suggested in the final pages of this book when I wrote it four years ago.

Yes, we keep learning and since starting the Spiritually Aware Parenting writing journey I have learnt so much. This book was the launching place of a new career path, a new focus, a new way of thought and a new way of living for me. I have had trials and errors, I have researched and read, I have taken part in discussions and helped many find peaceful solutions. Suddenly, I found I felt off about some issues in the book and they needed amending.

So finally, in the concept of feeling good, I've done some of the necessary edits. I didn't like the niggly feeling it was giving me. Have I covered them all? Possibly not, but enough of them.

I think on the whole I wish it conveyed one thing maybe more than it does, something my subsequent books cover better and the unwritten ones will express the best, Life is Magic. Nothing in this illusion is real and it is all miraculous. Parenting can tie us into knots as we contort into unimaginable positions trying to give our children everything. But when we relax, breathe, laugh and remember that worrying is only using our imaginations for unhappy outcomes, we can shift our thoughts and in doing so, shift reality.

Energy, vibration, feeling space, they are all different ways of expressing that life is made up of a magical concept of sense. The way we focus our thoughts, creates a diffcrent magic. The way we perceive our world, our days and our children, creates the environment surrounding us.

Chose to see the best, and you will feel the best. Scientifically, positive thought is proven to create a space to see more options, to see solutions. Close off energy with negative thought, and we tend to tread water in our own misery. Therefore, although it seems illogical, trust the magic. If you are having a bad day, find something to feel better about and a solution will find you.

This book was meant to be the first of a two part series. The second book is yet to be written. I had things to learn, life to absorb, before I could put them to paper. It's almost there.

In the meantime, be well dear friends. You are so special and so are your children. We come at a great time and your children have chosen you well. They knew you could offer them the greatest of love, the companionship of understanding and the ability to grow and learn. Trust in it and thrive.

In love and light,

Christina

Who They Really Are

www.ingramcontent.com/pod-product-compliance
Lightning Source LLC
Chambersburg PA
CBHW032119090426
42743CB00007B/393